John Wesley Hoyt

**Memorial in Regard to a National University**

John Wesley Hoyt

**Memorial in Regard to a National University**

ISBN/EAN: 9783337035907

Printed in Europe, USA, Canada, Australia, Japan

Cover: Foto ©ninafisch / pixelio.de

More available books at **www.hansebooks.com**

# NATIONAL UNIVERSITY,

BY

## JOHN W. HOYT.

WASHINGTON:
GOVERNMENT PRINTING OFFICE,
1892,

# CONTENTS.

# ACTION OF THE SENATE.

Mr. PROCTOR. I present the memorial of Hon. John W. Hoyt in regard to a National University, with an accompanying document, which is a very valuable historical statement on that subject. I move that it be printed and referred to the Select Committee to Establish the University of the United States.

The motion was agreed to.

Mr. SHERMAN. I move that 5,000 extra copies of the document be printed for the use of the Senate, and that the motion be referred to the Committee on Printing.

*     *     *     *     *     *     *     *     *     *

The VICE-PRESIDENT. Will the Senator from Ohio please repeat his statement? The Chair did not hear it.

Mr. SHERMAN. The Senator from Vermont presented a memorial accompanied by a very valuable document in regard to the National University and moved that it be referred to the committee on that subject, of which I happen to be a member, and printed. I move that 5,000 extra copies may be printed for the use of the Senate. I do not know what it will cost to print that number. I ask that the motion to print extra copies be referred to the Committee on Printing.

The VICE-PRESIDENT. That order will be made in the absence of objection.

Mr. MANDERSON, from the Committee on Printing, to whom was referred the following resolution, reported it without amendment, and it was considered by unanimous consent and agreed to:

*Ordered,* That 5,000 additional copies of the memorial of John W. Hoyt in relation to the establishment of the University of the United States, with the accompanying paper, be printed for the use of the Senate.

# MEMORIAL.

WASHINGTON, D. C., *August 3, 1892.*

*To the Honorable the Senate of the United States:*

Responding to the request of the chairman of the Select Committee to Establish the University of the United States, for an account of what has been done hitherto in support of the proposition to found a national university in this country, together with a statement of what is now deemed desirable in this behalf from the standpoint of such eminent citizens and national organizations as are committed to that enterprise, I have the honor to submit the accompanying paper, and pray that the same may be printed in the usual number and referred to the aforesaid committee.

Very respectfully,

JOHN W. HOYT.

13

# A NATIONAL UNIVERSITY.

The subject of a national university has received much attention among thoughtful and patriotic citizens in all periods of our national history.

Thus far, the main hindrances to the enterprise have been, less than a just appreciation of its importance by the masses of the people, coupled with the early prevalence of provincial ideas and local jealousies, besides more or less doubt concerning the constitutional powers of the Government and a supreme devotion to the work of material development, on the one hand, and on the other a misapprehension of the relation that would be sustained by a central and truly national university to existing institutions of the university class.

The first of these embarrassments, though somewhat slow to disappear, is now rapidly passing away. With the spread of educational facilities, the growth of institutions for the higher culture, the marvelous progress of science and learning, and the consequent increase of those discoveries, practical inventions, and literary achievements, which have greatly added to the pleasures, security, and dignity of life, there has also come a new recognition of the high value of learn. ing; so that intelligent citizens everywhere now vie with each other in their efforts to promote its advancement. Even the uncultured have learned the theory of a necessary connection between science and progress in the useful arts, and hence, for their own immediate good, as well as for the advantage of their children and for the general welfare, willingly bear a share of the light burden necessary to the upbuilding and maintenance of the higher institutions.

So, too, with the construction of numberless railways and the constant intermingling of the people of all sections, provincialism has died a natural death. Each community has learned not only to respect every other, but to find pleasure in the prosperity of all as portions of a common country.

Moreover, as a result of what has been done by the Federal Government for the safety, convenience, and progress of all, those larger views now prevail which have made us one people, more loyal than ever to the Constitution, yet wisely regarding it, as did the framers themselves, an instrument formed with a view to national development and to high rank among the nations as well as to the preservation of our liberties.

Finally, there is reason to believe that the hindrance last mentioned will yet more quickly vanish when it comes to be understood at the educational centers that the real purpose of the friends of the proposed university is not to build up a powerful rival to existing institutions, but rather, first, to supplement the instruction the college now gives in its graduate courses with the highest and fullest post-graduate teaching the world can furnish, and, secondly, to supply such facilities for original work under the guidance of master minds as are still so greatly needed, and as would enable it incidentally to supply all the collegiate institutions of the land with persons most competent to fill their chairs of instruction, in return for the multitude of bachelors of arts, letters, science, and philosophy that would flock to the national standard.

One can hardly conceive of a more powerful and effective agency than such an institution would be, whether for the uplifting of the schools of the whole country of every class and grade, for the advancement of science and learning in the world, or for giving to the United States a true intellectual supremacy among the nations of the earth.

In view of all these facts and considerations the general question of establishing some such central university should now find an easy and ready solution.   Hence this new revival of it, and this further appeal to the Congress of the United States, with a statement of what should be deemed requisite in this regard, of what has been attempted in that direction heretofore, and of what may reasonably be expected of both people and Government in the interest of science and learning, and as a crowning act of this first full century of the national life.

# I.

## OFFICES OF A TRUE UNIVERSITY.

While the term university has had so great a variety of applications that it is practically without definiteness of meaning, it is nevertheless manifest that it has a proper signification as well as application. Stating these as simply as possible by defining the offices which such an institution may be expected to fulfil, it is hardly necessary to say, first of all, that it ranks above and beyond the academic and collegiate institutions, those stepping stones by which it is conveniently reached, or that its applicants for admission should have completed the courses of instruction which those classes of schools offer, and have fully gained both the priceless discipline and the very moderate attainments in knowledge which they represent.

The studies therein mastered are supposed to have simply furnished a key with which, if intellectually capable and of resolute purpose, they who have been certificated by them may enter those vastly broader and higher fields of science, art, and philosophy which themselves border on infinity.

As the common schools of this country, broadly viewed, represent what is elementary in the processes of development and acquisition, so the college properly stands for what is secondary, leaving all beyond as the realm of the true university. This is well understood by those who stand at the head of the multitude of so-called universities in America. They do not need to be told of the deficiencies they represent. They are simply willing to let their growing schools for the present bear the high title of which they anxiously hope to make them some day worthy.

Following the example of the German universities, several of our greater institutions have bravely thrown their forces across the line and are doing a large amount of the very best of university work; but the bulk of work still done in the majority of such as bear the university name is the work of the college—the preparation of youth for the degree of bachelor.

The university proposed will open its doors for regular courses with graduation to such only as are at least bachelors already—eventually to multitudes of such as have been honored with even the doctor's degree, since it will be able to furnish to each and to all the very ultimate of what has been achieved in every realm and department of learning.

It will be not simply one more of the vast number of schools of academic rank, but the crown and culmination of the now incomplete American system of education—a flowering of the magnificent growth we have been nursing through sunshine and storm these more than a hundred years.

S. Mis. 222——2

A second office of the university is that of forming a complete circle of schools of corresponding grade for each and all of the recognized professions—not schools limited, like those of the present, to that modicum of attainments which barely represents the bachelor's degree, but rather such as, beginning with the bachelor's grade, would meet the demands of students aspiring to the highest possible attainments in their respective departments, and confer degrees in none of lower rank than those of master and doctor.

Thirdly, a university of this high character, doing post-graduate work in its central departments and in all other fields now occupied in any efficient manner by existing institutions, could properly perform still another function, that of building new professions, as justified in so doing, on the basis of known facts and established principles, by opening proper courses of study therein; thus lifting the so-called occupations and trades out of the domain of empiricism into the high realm of science.

A fourth office of a true university is that of enlarging the field of human knowledge by means of the researches and investigations of its professors and fellows. Thus far this high function has been but partially performed anywhere. And yet how inconceivably great are the possibilities of an institution not only ever at the front in its mastery of all that is known, nor yet by its members of genius ever at work on new problems in every realm and department of the material, intellectual, and moral universe, and making new discoveries in aid of further progress, but also in a truly philosophic manner teaching its members the very art and science of investigation itself.

In an important sense this last-named function of the university is to be its leading one; for an institution wholly, or even very seriously, deficient in this exalted role would in no proper sense be a university at all. With the utmost completeness in all other respects there would still remain an aching void. An insatiable spirit of inquiry, an unquenchable ambition to advance the boundaries of human knowledge by new conquests in the infinite realm of the unknown, must pervade and will pervade an institution deserving the high title of university. It can instruct, elevate, coördinate, and originate effectively, only in proportion as it entitles itself to the confidence of the learned and scientific world by its sure command of all the heights and outposts, nay, in proportion as by its high courage, restless energy and skill, it adds to the sum total of human achievement.

Finally, it is an important office of such a university to defend, as well as determine, the truth. Among its members there will always be moral heroes as superior to the menaces of power as to the insidious arts of the most skillful and corrupt devotees of false gods—men able to unmask error and bold to stand for the right at all hazards. The sacredness of truth, freedom of thought, and freedom of speech will be the inscription upon its portals. It will be not a light-house only, but also a bulwark of liberty and a watch-tower for the nation and the world.

# II.

## REASONS FOR FOUNDING A NATIONAL UNIVERSITY.

First of all, the task of planting and endowing a true university is herculean, requiring an amount of means not hitherto furnished nor likely to be furnished without the help of the nation. Great munificence has been practiced here and there in recent years by noble-hearted Americans, whose gifts have far eclipsed the benefactions of all other countries and times; but the endowments thus accorded, besides being insufficient, are ever liable to be in some manner restricted, so as more or less to embarrass the administration of them. Moreover, in the nature of the case they usually, if not invariably, somewhat limit or prevent subsequent benefactions to the same end by the very terms of the donation and the naming of the institution.

On the other hand, the United States, richest, most powerful, and most progressive of all the nations, could easily confer such an endowment on an institution of its own founding as to make it very soon foremost in all the world in point of resources and possibilities.

Nor is this all; the very giving to it the stamp of the nation, with means enough to insure its supremacy, so far from deterring any other giver, would operate as a powerful incentive to all persons of fortune desirous of promoting any kind of instruction or any line of investigation by affording every assurance of security and permanency of the institution itself, by offering them the opportunity of connecting their benefactions and names enduringly with the most important, as well as most brilliant, cluster of schools on the earth, and by giving them to realize that high sense of dignity and honor which must attach to a permanent copartnership with the Government in an undertaking of the highest character possible to man or to nations of men.

Secondly, that a national university of this sort would meet a vital want of American education, by supplying the head and culmination it lacks, is too manifest to require argument. At present we have a series of schools in the States quite complete, beginning with the kindergarten and ending with the university. But there the work of building has rested even until now. Viewed in all its relations and obligations, the proudly-styled "American system" is a truncated pyramid. A national post-graduate university is therefore a logical necessity. Without it our youth must stop short of the full measure of learning and discipline to which they aspire, or seek for them wholly outside. Nor is this all; without the final, supreme institution the whole series lacks the immeasurable advantage that would come of a complete coördination of all grades from the lowest to the highest, so that each link in the series below would be controlled and lifted by the regulating power of the highest, exercised through the fixing of its own standards of admission; this, to say nothing of the further incalculable gain of having such a supreme institution as a constant source of supply for teachers of the highest qualifications to be found in the world.

But, thirdly, it is more than a logical necessity from the standpoint of a complete systematic scheme; it is also a patriotic necessity. It is only a national university that could in the most eminent degree cultivate, strengthen, and fortify that sentiment of patriotism on which the security and future glory of the American Republic must depend. It was this consideration, next to the interests of learning, that so weighed with Washington that he never forgot it in his eloquent appeals to his countrymen.

The gathering of youthful persons of character and scholarship from every quarter of the country, for association on the high plane of the university for a period of years, would not only make them fellows socially and in things intellectual; it would also powerfully tend to strengthen the patriotism of each and all; first by an increase of their respect, admiration, and affection for a government at once wise and so beneficent, and, secondly, by the promotion of lasting friendships among a class of representatives of diverse sections of the country certain to be among the most influential of their citizens, as well as potential leaders of thought and sentiment in the country at large. Possibly the present greatness of our own country, with the marked progress of some of our foremost institutions, may have diminished the force of Washington's argument as to the influence of foreign associations in weakening the patriotism of our sons who were obliged to cross the ocean for the best facilities for study; but, on the other hand, that very greatness has become an unanswerable reason why America should now herself provide educational opportunities proportioned to her relative importance, her undeniable supremacy among the nations.

The country will cordially welcome such contributions to this end as the churches, or any of them, are pleased to make, but it is hardly conceivable that a great nation whose aspirations look to ascendancy not only in wealth and power but also in those noble achievements which are conditioned on preëminence of the higher culture, should so neglect its duty as to leave this vital interest to even the best attempts of competing religious organizations, or to voluntary agencies of any sort whatsoever. The duty of the nation to meet this demand on its own account, and to meet it most thoroughly, is a solemn duty. It may not be shirked, and should not be longer postponed.

Again, it is only a university with a base as broad as the nation itself, aye, as broad as universal truth, that could hope to draw upon the sympathies and upon the moral as well as material resources of the whole

American people. A university founded on denominational preferences, or any other preferences, is by that very fact largely limited in its patronage to the great family of faith to which it belongs. It can not win all alike by the banner it floats. Nor can such an institution, however pure and lofty its aims, free itself utterly, if it would, from preferring that all who come to it for any purpose should accept the particular faith it represents. A national university need not be, and would not be, devoid of religious sentiment, since that is something which inheres in the individual soul, but it could have no special shibboleth, no banner but that of truth and virtue. To its halls all truth-seekers would be alike welcome. The great American nation owes the founding of an unbiased, independent, and truly national university to the sacred cause of impartial truth and justice. It must not force its sons and daughters of genius to enter less than the broadest as well as most exalted temple of learning that can be established with the help of unstinted resources and the highest available wisdom.

And again, the American nation owes it to the cause of republican liberty to establish such a university; since, if established, it would not only help to strengthen our own bands, but, through the influence of men of genius who would come to it from all parts of the world, become a powerful indirect means of promoting the growth of free institutions in other lands.

Finally, a great nation like ours has resting upon it the solemn obligation to contribute in large measure to the advancement of knowledge as a means of general human progress. To this end such a university would contribute to a degree beyond the power of calculation. Discoveries and inventions of every sort would greatly multiply under the force of its inspiration and systematic direction. As a consequence, the burden of toil would be earlier lightened in all civilized lands; added millions of unfettered minds would earlier find new profit as well as pleasure in the world of thought; and mankind would advance with more rapid strides towards the goal of a true civilization. Hence it was that the patriots and philanthropists of America but lately gathered in Independence Hall, for the organization of a human freedom league and for the purpose of maturing plans for a congress of the representatives of all the republics, adopted resolutions strongly supportive of the proposition to found a national university at the earliest possible day.

# III.

## REASONS FOR THE UNIVERSITY AT WASHINGTON.

These are not far to seek. In the first place, the District of Columbia is the only sufficient and suitable spot within the United States where the Federal Government has exclusive and perpetual jurisdiction.

Secondly, the District of Columbia, besides being in every way suitable as a location, is the spot designated by the Father of his Country, who was the first to propose its establishment, and who left such endowment as he was able for its establishment there.

Moreover, Washington is far more than a "sufficient and suitable" spot for a national university.

(1) It is built in the midst of one of the finest landscapes in America—one that becomes to the lover of nature a constant source of pleasure and inspiration.

(2) It is one of the most healthful, as well as most agreeable, localities in the country—warm enough in summer, yet never so hot as some others, never intensely cold in winter; its climate, all in all, more equable than that enjoyed by other cities east of the Rocky Mountains.

(3) The city of Washington is without parallel in this country for the excellence of its plan; for the number of its parks, squares, triangles, and circles; for the breadth and beauty of its streets, the magnificence of its public structures, and the extent of its adornment with historic monuments and the statues of heroic men.

(4) It abounds in historic associations of priceless value. One sees on every hand the private abodes and places for public activity of statesmen, orators, scholars, and scientists who have won immortal honors and added unfading luster to the American name.

(5) As the city stands to-day it is hardly equaled by any other for the elegance of its private mansions; and the building of new ones, each vieing with the other, still proceeds at a steady if not rapid pace.

(6) It is a desirable place for the residence of advanced students and professors, because of the unequaled proportion of its citizens eminent for culture in science, art, letters, and philosophy.

(7) It is no less desirable on account of its metropolitan character. Here are gathered annually and almost constantly leading representatives of all geographical divisions; not only the statesmen of all sections, but also the representatives of every sort of national organiza-

22

tion. It is fast becoming the rallying point for every great interest of the country and the world.

(8) With its varied culture and elegance of manners, it is also the most democratic of cities. Men and women of worth and genius, whose modest means and humble abode would limit them in some other cities to the more lowly associations, are here made welcome in the costly palace of the cultured and opulent.

(9) The multitude of religious, charitable, and philanthropic organizations in active operation, with less than the average proportion of the haunts of vice, make it a comparatively safe place for advanced students whose ambition would lead them to Washington as a high seat of learning.

(10) For all these reasons—for what Washington is, embraces, and represents—there is no place like it in America for the culture and sure growth of a love of country. The students here gathered from every quarter, and here taught, not alone by the university, but likewise taught and molded by the spirit and patriotic influences of the city itself, would in time return to their thousands of homes more ardent patriots, the better qualified to serve their country, the more resolute in purpose to protect it from perils of every nature and to promote its highest welfare.

Thirdly, Washington has already an aggregation of facilities and opportunities in the way of legislative bodies, courts of every class, scientific bureaus, and like organizations, as well as libraries, museums, art collections, laboratories, workshops, and other sources of help available to a greater or less extent, such as is hardly surpassed by any in even the Old World. Behold the inventory of them:

In the Treasury Department of the United States—
    The Office of the Coast and Geodetic Survey.
    The Office of the Life-Saving Service.
    The Marine Hospital Service.
    The Bureau of Statistics.
    The Bureau of Engraving and Printing.
In the War Department—
    The several military bureaus.
In the Navy Department—
    The Naval Observatory.
    The Office of the Nautical Almanac.
    The Hydrographic Office.
    The Bureau of Navigation.
    The Bureau of Yards and Docks.
    The Bureau of Ordnance.
    The Bureau of Construction and Repair.
    The Bureau of Steam Engineering.
    The Museum of Hygiene.
    The Bureau of Medicine and Surgery.
    The Dispensary.

In the Department of the Interior—
  The Patent Office.
  The Bureau of Education.
  The Office of the Geological Survey.
  The Census Office.
In the Department of Agriculture—
  The Botanical Division, with the gardens and grounds.
  The Division of Vegetable Pathology.
  The Pomological Division.
  The Microscopical Division.
  The Chemical Division.
  The Ornithological Division.
  The Forestry Division.
  The Entomological Division.
  The Silk Section.
  The Experimental Stations.
  The Office of Statistics.
  The Bureau of Animal Industry.
  The Weather Bureau.
  The Agricultural Museum.
Of establishments not under Departmental control—
  The Smithsonian Institution.
  The National Museum, with its twenty-two departments.
  The Medical Museum.
  The Medical Library.
  The Bureau of Ethnology.
  The Light-House Board.
  The Commission of Fish and Fisheries.
  The Arsenal.
  The Congressional Library.
  The United States Botanic Garden.
  The Zoölogical Garden (in preparation).
  The Government Printing Office.
  The Soldiers' Home.
  Office of the National Board of Health.
  Government Hospital for the Insane.
  The National Deaf-Mute College.
  Courts, District, Circuit, and Supreme.
Of local institutions and establishments—
  The Columbian University, with its professional department of
    law and department of medicine.
  The Howard University, with its like departments.
  The Georgetown University, with its departments.
  The "National University" law school and school of medicine.
  The Corcoran Art Gallery.
  The Columbia Institution for the Deaf and Dumb.

Of local institutions and establishments—Continued.

The Columbia Hospital for Women.

The Children's Hospital.

The Providence Hospital.

Of learned associations of men—

The Philosophical Society of Washington.

The Anthropological Society.

The Biological Society.

The Chemical Society.

The Botanical Society.

The National Geographical Society.

To all of which might be added, since their annual meetings are held at Washington, the National Academy of Sciences, and the American Historical Society.

Already the total valuation of the collections, literary and scientific, belonging to the Government and available for purposes of instruction, is over $30,000,000; the aggregate expenditures for the care and use of them in the work of the Government, nearly $4,000,000 annually. And the collections are rapidly growing.

The Congressional Library, already the largest in the New World, having long since outgrown its present accommodations, is soon to be put in possession of the finest library building on the face of the earth and will then rapidly advance to its proper rank by the side of those great collections at London and Paris.

The Smithsonian Institution, having relations of exchange with every government, institution, and society of importance in the world, is prepared to offer to the University, when established, unparalleled advantages in the departments of natural history and the arts.

Fourth. We have at Washington, in all departments of the Government, nearly a thousand experts in a great number of classes or branches of service, from the shops in the navy-yard to the Supreme Court itself; the whole body of them constituting the most important cluster of men of genius and rare attainments in the world. Hundreds of these men could serve a great university, either as lecturers and instructors, or by furtherance of its scientific work in some other way; thus greatly aiding it, while also adding something to their very moderate regular incomes, and gaining new inspiration for a still better service in their usual rounds, if not, indeed, for the supreme work of new discovery. For a great and powerful nation to allow all these vast and varied resources to remain indefinitely without the fullest possible use in the interest of science and learning, while at the same time multitudes of its citizens are suffering irreparable loss for want of them, is incomprehensible. It is certainly the worst economy conceivable and seems hardly less than criminal.

Fifth. Washington is becoming not only the most beautiful large city in America, as well as one of the most healthful, and also a favorite place of residence for people of talent, culture, and fortune; it is also to be the seat of many institutions of learning; adding to the universities already there, with the several law and other professional schools, which have made it an important educational center, great institutions of the university rank for the Catholic and Methodist churches, and probably for yet other religious bodies. Plant there, in the midst of all these, a national university, with its great central faculties of art, letters, science, and philosophy, its high departments of the mathematical and physical sciences, of applied chemistry, of mining and metallurgy, of civil and mechanical engineering, of topographical and hydrographical engineering, of architecture, of geology and mineralogy, of the biological sciences, of agriculture, of sanitation, of medicine, of jurisprudence, of education, of commerce, of the social and political sciences, with its superior schools of every other sort, bringing into relations with it the navy and military schools as well, and there will also come the great theological schools of every denomination, each with its independent control, yet each borrowing from the university in many departments, and in turn strengthening it by augmentation of numbers consecrated to high aims, and giving to it that increased invigoration which comes of the attrition of intellectual forces.

Sixth. Since Washington is the seat of government for the nation, it is for the interest of good government that the representatives of the people who concentrate there should have the benefit of such an atmosphere and of such personal contact as would be afforded by a university city. Larger information, broader views, and loftier aims would be theirs, even the ablest and best of them, by reason of the influences that would envelop them even as the earth is enveloped in its own ocean of ether.

Seventh. The presence of a great university in the national capital would have a direct influence on the character of the people's representation in Congress; encouraging men of the highest type, of highest culture, and of purest aspirations to seek these positions of so great importance to the country and to the cause of good government everywhere, and yet from which some may now shrink because of the sacrifices involved.

Last of all, the presence of a great national university at the seat of government, with all it involves of opportunity, intellectual association, social refinement, and moral dignity, would tend to insure to the United States such representation from foreign courts as would yet further improve the tone of the national capital, while in an important manner adding to the influence of our country in all matters of diplomatic intercourse and in the satisfactory adjustment of international questions.

# IV.

## SUMMARY OF EFFORTS IN THE PAST.

A summary of the notable efforts hitherto made in behalf of a national university would probably surprise even those most familiar with the history of education. While it can hardly be doubted that others than those herein noted have been made, it is nevertheless true that great care has been taken to make the memorandum complete, and to present the steps known to have been taken in due chronological order, beginning with the few important words to that end in Gen. Washington's headquarters at Cambridge, and ending with the resolutions recently adopted by the Human Freedom League in old Independence Hall, and by the General Committee of Three Hundred charged with the duty of arranging for a Pan-Republic Congress, to be held in 1893.

Passing such known efforts in simple review, we note:

I. The suggestion of Samuel Blodget, afterwards author of the first formal American work on political economy, in the presence of Gen. Washington, Gen. Greene, and Maj. William Blodget, in Washington's military camp at Cambridge, in October, 1775—a suggestion made in answer to remarks upon the damage the militia were doing to the colleges in which they were quartered, and in the following words:

> Well, to make amends for these injuries, I hope after our war we shall erect a noble *national university* at which the youth of all the world may be proud to receive instructions.[1]

II. The important words of Gen. Washington in response to the foregoing, namely:

> *Young man, you are a prophet, inspired to speak what I am confident will one day be realized.*

III. The yet more memorable remark of Washington after the Revolutionary war, the permanent location of the national capital, and a most careful consideration of the university interest, to wit:

> While the work of establishing a national university may be properly deferred until Congress is comfortably accommodated and the city has so far grown as to be prepared for it, the *enterprise must not be forgotten; and I trust that I have not omitted to take such measures as will at all events secure the entire object in time.* (Referring to his intended bequest.)

IV. The strenuous efforts of James Madison and Charles C. Pickering, doubtless with the earnest encouragement of Washington, and with

---

[1] Samuel Blodget's "Economica," p. 22.

the active support of Benjamin Franklin, James Wilson, William Samuel Johnson, James Rutledge, and yet others of its distinguished members, in the Constitutional Convention of 1787, who desired to have provision for a national university expressly made in the Constitution itself—efforts only at length discontinued in deference to the general opinion that the power to establish such an institution was sufficiently implied.

Following is a correct summary of the proceedings on this subject in the convention, as recorded by James Madison:

*May 29, 1787.*—Mr. Charles Pickering laid before the House the draft of a Federal Government, which he had prepared, to be agreed upon between the free and independent States of America:

The legislature shall have power  *  *  *

*  *  *  *  *  *  *

To establish and provide for a national university at the seat of government of the United States.[1]

*  *  *  *  *  *  *

*August 18, 1787.*—In convention Mr. Madison submitted, in order to be referred to the Committee of Detail, the following powers proposed to be added to those of the general legislature:

*  *  *  To establish a university.[2]

*  *  *  *  *  *  *

*September 14, 1787.*—Mr. Madison and Mr. Pickering moved to insert in the list of powers voted in August a power to establish a university in which no preference or distinction should be allowed on account of religion.[3]

Mr. Wilson and others supported the motion, but Gouverneur Morris strongly insisted that such addition to the Constitution would be a superfluity, since "the exclusive power at the seat of government would reach the object." This view was shared by enough members to defeat the proposition; Pennsylvania, Virginia, North Carolina, South Carolina, and Mr. Johnson, of Connecticut, voting for it as a means of making the university more sure, and Massachusetts, New Hampshire, New Jersey, Delaware, Maryland, Georgia, and Mr. Sherman, of Connecticut, voting in the negative. Not one word appears to have been said against the desirability of the proposed university.

V. The argument and appeal of Dr. Benjamin Rush, signer of the Declaration of Independence and a leading scientist of his time:

(1) In his address to the people of the United States, in 1787, among other things, strongly arguing for a Federal university, as a means of securing to the people an education suited to the needs of the country, a true university with post-graduate scholarships, and fellowships in connection with the consular service, and an educated civil service generally.

(2) A year later, in another appeal through the Pennsylvania Gazette, in which are found the following passages:

Your government can not be executed; it is too extensive for a republic. It is contrary to the habits of the people, say the enemies of the Constitution of the United States. However opposite to the opinions and wishes of a majority of the citizens

[1] Madison Papers, II, 740.   [2] Madison Papers, III, 1354.   [3] Madison Papers, III, 1577.

of the United States these declarations and predictions may be, they will certainly come to pass, unless the people are prepared for our new form of government by an education adapted to the new and peculiar situation of our country. To effect this great and necessary work let one of the first acts of the new Congress be to establish within the district to be allotted for them, a Federal university, into which the youth of the United States shall be received after they have finished their studies and taken degrees in the colleges of their respective States. * * *

Should this plan of a Federal university, or one like it, be adopted, then will begin the golden age of the United States. While the business of education in Europe consists in lectures upon the ruins of Palmyra and the antiquities of Herculaneum, or in dispute about Hebrew points, Greek particles, or the accent and quantity of the Roman language, the youth of America will be employed in acquiring those branches of knowledge which increase the convenience of life, lessen human misery, improve our country, promote population, exalt the human understanding, and establish domestic, social, and political happiness.

Let it not be said, This is not the time for such a literary and political establishment. Let us first restore public credit. * * * Let us regulate our militia, let us build our navy, and let us protect and extend our commerce. * * * This is false reasoning. We shall never restore public credit, regulate our militia, build a navy, or revive our commerce until we remove the ignorance and prejudices and change the habits of our citizens, and this can never be done until we inspire them with Federal principles, which can only be effected by our young men meeting and spending two or three years together in a national university, and afterwards disseminating their knowledge and principles through every county, town, and village of the United States.—[Republished by Dr. Goode, 1790.]

VI. The efforts of the newspaper press during the closing years of the last century, as reported by Samuel Blodget in his work entitled "Economica"—efforts so many that in speaking of them he remarks:

It would be an endless task, and require volumes to hold all that has been written in favor of a Federal heart and university in our perodical papers since 1775.

As examples, extracts are taken from some of the newspaper articles quoted by Blodget[1] as published September, 1787.

If a Federal university should be established I shall advance my humble opinion on the plan; here it is enough to observe that the institution must be simple, complete, and grand. The great science of politics requires a particular professorship, and a person qualified for this place must be one of the first characters in the United States. A mere financier or civilian is not a politician; this philosophic character must understand morals, war, finance, commerce, manufactures, agriculture, police, philosophy; he must have a perfect view of all the great affairs of a nation in their whole extent and intimate connection. * * *

The belles lettres or elegant literature claim also particular attention. These are both in the ancient and modern stile called humaniora, because they humanize and refine the human heart. They are not merely ornamental, but extremely useful in ennobling those affections which are the bands of civil society; and by qualifying men in several respects for all the important offices of government. * * *

Natural philosophy and mathematics are the same everywhere, but moral and sentimental literature has a great influence on manners and government. A critical inquiry into the species and forms of learning most proper for America would be a noble object to a man of genius and political knowledge. * * *

America must have her own sterling, even in learning; *let her establish an academy of belles lettres;* of this every fine genius in the Union should be a member; it must be central, and under the patronage of the Federal power.

[1] Economica, Appendix, pp. IV-VII.

From the Independent Gazetteer, Philadelphia, 1788. No. 548:

A gentleman under the signature of Nestor, some months since, gave the public a hint for erecting a Federal university. How much this will promote learning in general is evident from the situation of this young country, whose pecuniary and literary resources can not yet be great enough for more than one *illustrious assembly of the muses*. It would be an excellent institution for promoting Federal sentiments. In the happy spring of youth all our affections bloom—the high sense of honor, the warmth of friendship, the glow of patriotic virtue there animate the enraptured soul; sublime and elegant literature there has its highest relish, refines and exalts these noble passions. What glorious effects may not then a nation expect from a concourse of her best sons at the temple of wisdom! Society in the sweet enjoyment of wisdom, literature, and the many social pleasures of an academic life will create a mutual endearment and form those charming friendships that will continue to the grave. When after a finished education they depart to their different stations and places of residence they will be so many *capital links of the Federal Union;* so many stately columns under the grand fabric; so many bright luminaries to shed a radiance through the whole Federal system, and so many powerful centripetal forces to give eternal stability.

VII. In this connection may also be cited the following from The American Museum, October, 1789:

Whether viewed by the contemplative eye of the philosopher or fanned by the more active mind of the politician and legislator, the happiness arising to society from the progress of science in the world presents the most pleasing consequences as our encouragement to establish institutions for the education of youth in every branch of literature. No country is more indebted to the cause of learning than America. To the well-informed mind of her citizens does she owe her present important rank in the scale of nations; to this is she indebted for her unparalleled advances to greatness and empire, and on this does the preservation of her future liberties and all the invaluable rights of human nature essentially depend. * * *

America, from her local situation, possesses greater advantages for the promotion of literature and the arts than have marked any other nation in the early stages of its political existence, not being subject to the constant inroads of barbarians or the tyranny of superstition, nor interrupted by the frequent din of arms, ever hostile to the arts. * * *

While the lesser schools and every literary institution, however small, must be thought worthy the attention of Government, I hope to see the establishment of a Federal university. It is an idea which has been heretofore suggested, and which presages much future advantage to the public. Such a university may be erected in a central situation of the Union, under the management of able instructors, to which the students graduating at the different State colleges may repair to finish their education, by remaining two or three years, and principally directing their studies to the political interests of the country, the great object of legislation and national jurisprudence. As we have taken our station among the other nations of the world, it is highly proper we should form on national principles, which can be best done by promoting such institutions as have a tendency to remove local views and habits and beget mutual confidence, esteem, and good fellowship between those who * * * must rise or fall together. The institution above alluded to, I think, will be happily calculated to answer those valuable purposes and have the most beneficial effects in a political view. * * *

It remains for America, by an early attention to the encouragement of every art and science, and the cultivation of the human mind to the highest pitch of improvement, to fit the inhabitants of this western world for the enjoyment of that freedom and independence for which they have so nobly fought, and which will never be wrested from them while they imbibe with their milk the first principles. of civil liberty and are uniformly educated in an abhorrence of every attempt that may be formed to deprive them of this mighty boon of heaven.[1]

VIII. The words of President Washington in his address to Congress on January 8, 1790:

Nor am I less persuaded that you will agree with me in the opinion that there is nothing which can better deserve your patronage than the promotion of science and literature. Knowledge is, in every country, the surest basis of happiness. In one in which the measures of government receive their impressions so immediately from the sense of the community as in ours it is proportionably essential. To the security of a free constitution it contributes in various ways—by convincing those who are interested with the public administration that every valuable end of government is best answered by the enlightened confidence of the people and by teaching the people themselves to know and to value their own rights; to discern and provide against invasions of them; to distinguish between oppression and the necessary exercise of lawful authority, between brethren, proceeding from a disregard to their convenience, and those resulting from the inevitable exigencies of society; to discriminate the spirit of liberty from that of licentiousness, cherishing the first and avoiding the last; and uniting a speedy but temperate vigilance against encroachments with an inviolable respect for the laws. Whether this desirable object will be best promoted by affording aids to seminaries of learning already established, by the institution of a national university, or by any other expedients, will be worthy of a place in the deliberations of the legislature.[2]

IX. The Senate's concurring response of January 11, 1790, to President Washington's message of January 8, preceding.

Literature and science are essential to the preservation of a fair constitution; the measures of government should therefore be calculated to strengthen the confidence that is due to that important truth.[3]

X. The address of the House of Representatives, on January 12, 1790, in answer to the President's message of January 8.

We concur with you in the the sentiment that agriculture, commerce, and manufactures are entitled to legislative protection, and that the promotion of science and literature will contribute to the security of a free government. In the progress of our deliberations we shall not lose sight of objects so worthy of our regard.[4]

XI. President Washington's letter of November 27, 1794, to John Adams, Vice-President of the United States, relative to the proposition of Thomas Jefferson to import the Genevan faculty of learned men as a nucleus for a national university:

I have not been able to give the papers herewith enclosed more than a hasty reading, returning them without delay that you may offer the perusal of them to whomsoever you should think proper. The picture drawn in them of the Genevese is really interesting and affecting. The proposition of transplanting the members entire of the university of that place to America, with the acquisition of means to establish the same, and to be accompanied by a considerable emigration, is important, requiring more consideration than under the circumstances of the moment I am able to bestow upon it.

---

[1] American Museum, Vol. 6, pp. 290, 291.     [3] Id., p. 936.
[2] Annals of Congress, 1st Cong., 2d sess., p. 933.     [4] Id., p. 1052.

* That a national university in this country is a thing to be desired has always been my decided opinion, and the appropriation of ground and of lands for it in the Federal City has long been contemplated and talked of; but how matured or how far the transportation of an entire seminary of foreigners, who may not understand our language, can be assimilated therein is more than I am prepared to give an opinion upon, or indeed how far funds in either case are attainable. * * *

I shall at any leisure after the session is fairly opened take pleasure in a full and free consultation with you on the subject, being with much esteem and regard, etc.[1]

XII. President Washington's letter of December 15, 1794, to Edmund Randolph, Secretary of State, requesting his assistance, and that of Mr. James Madison, in maturing the measures proper to be adopted by him in disposing of the stocks designed to begin the endowment of the proposed national university:

For the reasons mentioned to you the other day, namely, the Virginia Assembly being in session, and a plan being on foot for establishing a seminary of learning upon an extensive scale in the Federal City, it would oblige me if you and Mr. Madison would endeavor to mature the measures which will be proper for me to pursue in order to bring my designs into view as soon as you can make it convenient to yourselves.

I do not know that the enclosed, or sentiments similar to them, are proper to be engrafted in the communications which are to be made to the legislature of Virginia, or to the gentlemen who are named as trustees of the seminary which is proposed to be established in the Federal City; but as it is an extract of what is contained in my will on this subject, I send it merely for consideration.

The shares in the different navigations are to be located and applied in the manner which has been the subject of conversation.[2]

XIII. Washington's formal letter of January 28, 1795, to the Commissioners of the District of Columbia, plainly announcing his intention to contribute a considerable sum towards the founding of a university peculiarly American in teachings; in which letter he said:

A plan for the establishment of a university in the Federal city has frequently been the subject of conversation. * * *

It has always been a source of serious reflection and sincere regret with me that the youth of the United States should be sent to foreign countries for the purpose of education. Although there are doubtless many, under these circumstances, who escape the danger of contracting principles unfavorable to republican government, yet we ought to deprecate the hazard attending ardent and susceptible minds from being too strongly and too easily prepossessed in favor of other political systems before they are capable of appreciating their own.

For this reason I have greatly wished to see a plan adopted by which the arts, sciences, and belles-lettres could be taught in their fullest extent, thereby embracing all the advantages of European tuition with the means of acquiring the liberal knowledge which is necessary to qualify our citizens for the exigencies of public as well as private life, and (which with me is a consideration of great magnitude) by assembling the youth from the different parts of this rising republic, contributing from their intercourse an interchange of information to the removal of prejudices which might perhaps sometimes arise from local circumstances.

The Federal city, from its centrality and the advantages which in other respects it must have over any other place in the United States, ought to be preferred as a

---

[1] Writings of Washington, Sparks, XI, 1.        [2] Id., p. 2.

proper site for such a university. And if a plan can be adopted upon a scale as extensive as I have described, and the execution of it should commence under favorable auspices in a reasonable time with a fair prospect of success, I will grant in perpetuity fifty shares in the navigation of the Potomac River toward the endowment of it.

What annuity will arise from these shares when the navigation is in full operation can at this time be only conjectured, and those who are acquainted with it can form as good a judgment as myself.

As the design of this university has assumed no form with which I am acquainted, and as I am equally ignorant who the persons are who have taken or are disposed to take the maturing of the plan upon themselves, I have been at a loss to whom I should make the communication of my intentions. If the Commissioners of the Federal city have any particular agency in bringing the matter forward, then the information which I now give to them is in proper course. If, on the other hand, they have no more to do in it than others who may be desirous of seeing so important a measure carried into effect, they will be so good as to excuse my using them as the medium for disclosing these my intentions; because it appears necessary that the funds for the establishment and support of the institution should be known to the promoters of it, and I see no mode more eligible for announcing my purpose. For these reasons I give you the trouble of this address, and the assurance of being, etc. [1]

XIV. The indirect approval of the national university proposition by Thomas Jefferson, in his letter of February 23, 1795, to Washington on the subject of transferring to this country the faculty of the College of Geneva, Switzerland, in which he said:

You were formerly deliberating on the purpose to which you should apply the shares in the Potomac and James River companies presented to you by our Assembly, and you did me the honor of asking me to think on the subject. As well as I remember, some academical institution was thought to offer the best application of the money. Should you have finally decided in favor of this, a circumstance has taken place which would render the present moment the most advantageous to carry it into execution by giving to it at the outset such an eclat and such solid advantage as would insure a very general concourse to it of the youths from all our States, and probably from the other parts of America, which are free enough to adopt it. The persecution which has taken place at Geneva has demolished the college of that place, which was, in a great measure, supported by the former government. The colleges of Geneva and Edinburg were considered as the two eyes of Europe in matters of science, insomuch that no other pretended to any rivalship with either. Edinburg has been the most famous in medicine during the life of Cullen; but Geneva most so in the other branches of science and much the most resorted to from the continent of Europe, because the French language was that which was used.

A Mr. D'Ivernois, a Genevan, and a man of science, known as the author of a history of that republic, has proposed the transplanting of that college in a body to America. He has written to me on the subject, as he has also done to Mr. Adams, as he was formerly known to us both, giving us the details of his views for effecting it. Probably these have been communicated to you by Mr. Adams, as D'Ivernois desired should be done, but lest they should not have been communicated, I will take the liberty of doing it. His plan, I think, would go to about ten or twelve professorships. He names to me the following professors as likely, if not certain, to embrace the plan. * * *

Sparks, XI, 14.

S. Mis. 222——3

It could not be expected that any proposition from strangers unacquainted with our means and our wants, could jump at once into a perfect accommodation with these. But those presented to us would seem to trend on and are capable of modifications reconcilable perhaps to the views of both parties.

(1) We can well dispense with her second and third colleges, the trial being too partial for our extensive country, and the second sufficiently and better provided for already by our public and private grammar schools. * * *

(2) We are not to count on raising the money from lands, and consequently we must give up the proposal of the colony of Geneva farmers. But the wealth of Geneva in money being notorious and the class of moneyed men being that which the new government are trying to get rid of, it is probable that a capital sum could be borrowed on the credit of the fund under consideration sufficient to meet the first expenses of the transplantation and establishment, and to supply also the deficiency of revenue till the profits of the shares shall become sufficiently superior to the support of the college to repay the sums borrowed.

(3) The composition of the academy can not be settled there. It must be adapted to our circumstances, and can therefore only be fixed between them and persons here acquainted with those circumstances, and conferring for the purpose after their arrival here. For a country so marked for agriculture as ours, I should think no professorship so important as one not mentioned by them—a professor of agriculture—who, before the students should leave the college, should carry them through a course of lectures on the principle and practice of agriculture; and that this professor should come from no country but England. Indeed, I should mark Young as the man to be obtained. These, however, are modifications to be left till their arrival here.

A question would arise as to the place of the establishment. As far as I can learn it is thought just that the State which gives the [first] revenue should be most considered in the uses to which it is appropriated. But I suppose that their expectations would be satisfied by a location within their limits, and that this might be so far from the Federal city as normal considerations would recommend, and yet near enough to it to be viewed as an appendage of that, and that the splendor of the two objects would reflect usefully on each other.

Circumstances have already consumed much of the time allowed us. Should you think the proposition can be brought at all within your views, your determination, as soon as more important occupations will admit of it, would require to be conveyed as early as possible to M. D'Ivernois. now in London, lest my last letter should throw the parties into other engagements.[1]

## XV. President Washington's letter of March 15, 1795, to Thomas Jefferson, in answer to inquiries of February 23:

I received your letter of the 23d ultimo, but not at so early a period as might have been expected from the date of it. My mind has always been more disposed to apply the shares in the inland navigation of the Potomac and James Rivers, which were left to my disposal by the Legislature of Virginia, towards the endowment of a university in the United States than to any other object it has contemplated. In pursuance of this idea, and understanding that other means are in embryo for establishing so useful a seminary in the Federal City, I did, on the 28th of January last, announce to the commissioners thereof my intention of vesting in perpetuity the fifty shares I held under that act in the navigation of the Potomac, as an additional means of carrying the plan into effect, provided it should be adopted on a scale so liberal as to extend to and embrace a complete system of education.

I had little hesitation in giving the Federal City a preference over all other places for the institution, for the following reasons: First, on account of its being the per-

[1] Sparks, XI, 473.

manent seat of the Government of this Union, and where the laws and policy of it must be better understood than in any local part thereof. Secondly, because of its centrality. Thirdly, because one-half (or near it) of the District of Columbia is within the commonwealth of Virginia, and the whole of the State not inconvenient thereto. Fourthly, because as a part of the endowment, it would be useful, but alone would be inadequate to that end. Fifthly, because many advantages, I conceive, would result from the jurisdiction which the general government will have over it, which no other spot would possess. And lastly, as the seminary is contemplated for the completion of education and study of the sciences, not for boys in their rudiments, it will afford the students an opportunity of attending the debates in Congress, and thereby becoming more liberally and better acquainted with the principles of law and government.

My judgment and my wishes point equally strong to the application of the James River shares to the same subject at the same place; but, considering the source from whence they were derived, I have, in the letter I am writing to the executive of Virginia on this subject, left the application of them to a seminary within the State, to be located by the legislature.

Hence, you will perceive that I have in a degree anticipated your proposition. I was restrained from going the whole length of the suggestion by the following considerations: First, I did not know to what extent or when any plan would be so matured for the establishment of a university, as would enable any assurances to be given to the application of M. D'Ivernois. Secondly, the propriety of transplanting the professors in a body (from Geneva) might be questioned for several reasons; among others, because they might not all be good characters nor all sufficiently acquainted with our language. And again, having been at variance with the leading party of their country, the measure might be considered as an aristocratical movement by more than those who, without any just cause that I can discover, are continually sounding the bell of aristocracy. And thirdly, because it might preclude some of the first professors in other countries from a participation, among whom some of the most celebrated characters in Scotland, in this line, might be obtained.

Something, but of what nature I am unable to inform you, has been written by Mr. Adams to M. D'Ivernois. Never having viewed my intended donation, as more than part of the means that were to set this establishment on foot, I did not incline to go too far in the encouragement of professors before the plan should assume a more formal shape, much less to induce an entire college to migrate. The enclosed is the answer I have received from the commissioners, from which, and the ideas I have here expressed, you will be enabled to decide on the best communication to be made to M. D'Ivernois. My letter to the commissioners has bound me to the fulfilment of what is therein engaged, and if the legislature of Virginia, on considering the subject, should view it in the same light as I do, the James River shares will be added threto, for I think one good institution of this sort is to be preferred to two imperfect ones, which, without other aid than the shares in both navigations, is more likely to fall through than to succeed upon the plan I contemplate, which is, in a few words, to supersede the necessity of sending the youth of this country abroad for the purpose of education, where too often the principles and habits unfriendly to republican government are imbibed, and not easily discarded. Instituting such a one of our own as will answer the end, and associating them in the same seminary, will contribute to wear off those prejudices and unreasonable jealousies which prevent or weaken friendships and impair the harmony of the Union. [1]

Mr. Jefferson himself was finally convinced of the impracticability of the D'Ivernois plan; and yet his interest in the national university increased with the years, as will appear from his official support as

---

[1] Sparks, xi, 19.

president. His heart was indeed set upon a university for Virginia, but he was nevertheless ready, and all the more ready, on that account to promote the founding of a culminating institution at Washington, to be established and maintained by the National Government.

XVI. President Washington's letter of March 16, 1795, to Governor Brooke, of Virginia, concerning the disposition to be made of the shares in the Potomac Company, finally accepted by him for public use:

It is with indescribable regret that I have seen the youth of the United States migrating to foreign countries in order to acquire the higher branches of erudition and to obtain a knowledge of the sciences. Although it would be injustice to many to pronounce the certainty of their imbibing maxims not congenial to republicanism, it must nevertheless be admitted that a serious danger is encountered by sending abroad among other political systems those who have not well learned the value of their own.

The time is therefore come when a plan of universal education ought to be adopted in the United States. Not only do the exigencies of public and private life demand it, but if it should ever be apprehended that prejudice would be entertained in one part of the Union against the other, an efficacious remedy will be to assemble the youth of every part under such circumstances as will, by freedom of intercourse and collision of sentiment, give to their minds the direction of truth, philanthropy, and mutual conciliation.

It has been represented that a university corresponding with these ideas is contemplated to be built in the Federal City, and that it will receive considerable endowments. This position is so eligible from its centrality, so convenient to Virginia, by whose legislature the shares were granted and in which part of the Federal District stands, and combines so many other conveniences, that I have determined to invest the Potomac shares in that university.

Presuming it to be more agreeable to the general assembly of Virginia that the shares in the James River Company should be assessed for a similar object in some part of that State, I intend to allot them for a seminary to be erected at such place as they shall deem most proper. I am disposed to believe that a seminary of learning upon an enlarged plan, but yet not coming up to the full idea of a university, is an institution to be preferred for the position which is to be chosen. The students who wish to pursue the whole range of science may pass with advantage from the seminary to the university, and the former by a due relation may be rendered coöperative with the latter.

I can not, however, dissemble my opinion that if all the shares were conferred on a university it would become far more important than when they are divided; and I have been constrained from concentring them in the same place merely by my anxiety to reconcile a particular attention to Virginia with a great good, in which she will abundantly share in common with the rest of the United States.

I must beg the favor of your excellency to lay this letter before that honorable body at their next session, in order that I may appropriate the James River shares to the place which they may prefer.[1]

XVII. The action of the Virginia legislature, on December 1, 1795, in responding to the foregoing communication of Washington to Governor Brooke.

(1) By passing at once the following resolutions, to wit:

Resolved, therefore, That the appropriation by the said George Washington of the aforesaid shares in the Potomac Company to the university intended to be erected

[1] Sparks, XI, 22.

in the Federal City is made in a manner most worthy of public regard, and of the approbation of this Commonwealth.

*Resolved also,* That he be requested to appropriate the aforesaid shares in the James River Company to a seminary at such place in the upper country as he may deem most convenient to a majority of the inhabitants thereof.[1]

### (2) By also declaring that—

The plan contemplated, of erecting a university in the Federal City, where the youth of the several States may be assembled and the course of their education finished, deserves the countenance and support of each State.

XVIII. The further argument for a university and the importance of its early establishment, contained in President Washington's letter of September 1, 1796, to Secretary of State Alexander Hamilton, wherein he expresses regret that the Secretary had deemed it advisable to omit from the farewell address, then in preparation, the reference to a national university, which he had seen fit to include in the rough draft sent to him; in which letter he said:

I mean education generally, as one of the surest means of enlightening and giving just views of thinking to our citizens, but particularly the establishment of a university, where the youth of all parts of the United States might receive the polish of erudition in the arts, sciences, and belles-lettres, and where those who were disposed to run a political course might not only be instructed in the theory and principles, but (this seminary being at the seat of the General Government where the legislature would be in session half the year, and the interests and politics of the nation would be discussed) would lay the surest foundation for the practical part also.

But that which would render it of the highest importance, in my opinion, is that at the juvenal period of life, when friendships are formed and habits established that stick by one, the youth or young men from different parts of the United States would be assembled together, and would by degrees discover that there was not that cause for those jealousies and prejudices which one part of the Union had imbibed against another. Of course sentiments of more liberality in the general policy of the country would result from it. What but the mixing of people from different parts of the United States during the war rubbed off these impressions? A century in the ordinary intercourse would not have accomplished what the seven years' association in arms did; but that ceasing, prejudices are beginning to revive again, and never will be eradicated so effectually by any other means as the intimate intercourse of characters in early life, who, in all probability, will be at the head of the counsels of this country in a more advanced stage it.

To show that this is no new idea of mine, I may appeal to my early communications to Congress, and to prove how seriously I have reflected on it since, and how well-disposed I have been and still am to contribute my aid towards carrying the measure into effect, I inclose you an extract of a letter from me to the governor of Virginia on this subject, and a copy of the resolutions of the legislature of that State in consequence thereof.

I have not the smallest doubt that this donation (when the navigation is in complete operation, which it will be in less than two years) will amount to 1,200 or 1,500 pounds sterling a year, and become a rapidly increasing fund. The proprietors of the Federal City have talked of doing something handsome towards it likewise, and if Congress would appropriate some of the western lands to the same uses funds sufficient and of the most permanent and increasing sort might be so established as to invite the ablest professors in Europe to conduct it.[2]

---

[1] Sparks, XI, 25, note.         [2] Works of Alex. Hamilton, VI, 147.

XIX. The second letter of Washington to the Secretary of State on this same subject, on September 6, 1796, in which, while acquiescing in the view of Hamilton, he not only confesses his doubt as to the wisdom of omitting his proposed national university paragraphs from the farewell address, but manifests anew, and more touchingly than elsewhere, his deep and abiding interest in the subject:

If you think that the idea of a university had better be reserved for the speech at the opening of the session, I am content to defer the communication of it until that period; but, even in that case, I would pray you, as soon as convenient, to make a draft for the occasion predicated on the ideas with which you have been furnished, looking, at the same time, into what was said on this head in my second speech to the first Congress, merely with a view to see what was said on the subject at that time; and this, you will perceive, was not so much to the point as I want to express now, though it may, if proper, be glanced at, to show that the subject had caught my attention early.

But, to be candid, I much question whether a recommendation of this measure to the legislature will have a better effect now than formerly. It may show, indeed, my sense of its importance, and that it is a sufficient inducement with me to bring the matter before the public in some shape or another at the closing scenes of my political exit. My object for proposing to insert it where I did (if not improper) was to set the people ruminating on the importance of the measure, as the most likely means of bringing it to pass.[1]

XX. Washington's Farewell Address, on September 17, 1796, wherein, without specializing upon this one particular point, on which he had, as above, spoken "once for all," he said:

Promote then, as a subject of primary importance, institutions for the general diffusion of knowledge. In proportion as the structure of government gives force to public opinion it is essential that public opinion shall be enlightened.[2]

XXI. Washington's letter to the commissioners of the Federal District, on October 21, 1796, announcing his final decision as to the grounds to be set apart for the purposes of the national university:

According to my promise I have given the several matters contained in your letter of the 1st instant the best consideration I am able.

The following is the result, subject, however, to alterations, if upon fuller investigation and the discussion I mean to have with you on these topics on my way to Philadelphia I should find cause therefor.[3]  [Designation of the lands chosen.]

XXII. The eighth annual message of President George Washington, delivered December 7, 1796, in which he said:

I have heretofore proposed to the consideration of Congress the expediency of establishing a national university and also a military academy. The desirableness of both these institutions has so constantly increased with every new view I have taken on the subject that I can not omit the opportunity of once for all recalling your attention to them. The assembly to which I address myself is too enlightened not to be fully sensible how much a flourishing state of the arts and sciences contributes to material prosperity and reputation. True it is that our country, much to its honor, contains many seminaries of learning highly respectable and useful; but the funds upon which they rest are too narrow to command the ablest professors, in the different departments of liberal knowledge, for the institution contemplated,

---

[1] Hamilton's Works, VI, 149, 150.    [3] Id., p. 322.

though they would be excellent auxiliaries. Among the motives to such an institution, the assimilation of the principles, opinions, and manners of our countrymen, by the common education of a port on of our youth from every quarter, will deserve attention. The more homogeneous our citizens can be made in these particulars, the greater will be our prospect of permanent union; and a primary object of such a national institution should be the education of our youth in the science of government. In a republic what species of knowledge can be equally important, and what duty more pressing on its legislature than to patronize a plan for communicating it to those who are to be the guardians of the future liberties of the country?[1]

XXIII. The approval of the proposition by the Senate of the United States, in its address of December 10, 1796, to President Washington, saying, as it did unanimously:

A national university may be converted to the most useful purposes; the science of legislation being so essentially dependent on the endowments of the mind, the public interests must receive effectual aid from the general diffusion of knowledge; and the United States will assume a more dignified station among the nations of the earth by the successful cultivation of the higher branches of learning.[2]

XXIV. The memorial of Gustavus Scott, William Thornton, and Alexander White, commissioners appointed under the "Act to establish the temporary and permanent seat of the Government of the United States," and to whom also was referred that part of the President's speech relating to a national university; said memorial presented on December 12, 1796, and being as follows, to wit:

*To the Honorable the Congress of the United States of America:*

The Commissioners appointed under the act entitled "An act for establishing the temporary seat of the Government of the United States," respectfully represent:

That the institution of a national university within the United States has been the subject of much conversation; that all men seem to agree in the utility of the measure, but that no effectual means have hitherto been proposed to accomplish it; that recent transactions seem to call upon them in a more particular manner than on their fellow-citizens at large to promote this desirable object; they therefore take the liberty to state that after the temporary and permanent seat of the Government of the United States was located by the President, agreeably to the act of Congress above mentioned, the proprietors of the lands adjacent to and including the sites designated for the public buildings ceded a large territory for the purpose of a Federal city, and by their deeds of cession authorized the President of the United States for the time being to appropriate such portions thereof as he should deem necessary to public use. In virtue of this power, the President has appropriated 19 acres 1 rood and 21 perches, part of the land so ceded, for the site of a national university. That he has likewise declared to them his intention to grant, in perpetuity, fifty shares in the navigation of the Potomac River as soon as the system assumes a shape which will enable him to do it with effect; and that they have no doubt when that event shall take place, but many liberal donations will be made as well in Europe as in America; that the money actually paid on these fifty shares is 5,000 pounds sterling; that the navigation is now nearly completed; and that all who are acquainted with the river Potomac and the adjacent country are sensible that the produce of these shares will be very great. They do not think it necessary to dilate on a subject in respect to which there seems to be but one voice.

The preservation of the morals and of the political principles of our youth; the savings of the expense of foreign education; the drawing to our shores the youth

---

[1] Annals, 4th Cong., 2d sess., p. 1519.    [2] Annals, 4th Cong., 2d sess., p. 1694.

of other countries, particularly those attached to republican government, and the proportionate accession of wealth; the removal, or at least the diminution, of those local prejudices which at present exist in the several States, by the uniformity of education, and the opportunity of a free interchange of sentiment and information among the youth from all the various points of the Union, which would consequently take place, may, with certainty, be accounted among the benefits resulting from such an institution. We flatter ourselves it is only necessary to bring this subject within the view of the Federal legislature. We think you will eagerly seize the occasion to extend to it your patronage, to give birth to an institution which may perpetuate and endear your names to the latest posterity.

How far it would be proper to go at the present moment we presume not to determine, but would beg leave to observe that, although the ultimate organization of the institution may be postponed to a future period, when the means of establishing and supporting it should be more fully ascertained, yet much good will arise from a law authorizing proper persons to receive pecuniary donations and to hold estates, real and personal, which may be granted by deed or devised by last will and testament, for the use of the intended establishment, with proper regulations for securing the due application of the moneys paid. Without some provisions of this kind (to the establishing of which we consider the Federal legislature alone competent) the benevolent wishes of the virtuous and well disposed will be rendered abortive.

Having performed what a sense of duty strongly impressed upon us to perform, we, with great respect, submit the consideration of the premises to your honorable body, with the further observation that the relative state of Europe and America seems to render this a favorable era for the commencement of the work. Whether the flames of war shall long continue to rage within the bounds of the former, or whether they shall be extinguished by a speedy peace, the learned and the wealthy in those unfortunate regions will seek an asylum from future oppression in our more happy country, many of whom will, no doubt, be among the foremost to promote those useful arts, the benefits of which they so well understand.[1]

In presenting the foregoing memorial Mr. Madison warmly indorsed the same:

Observing that it had been the subject of much conversation, but no effectual measures had been adopted toward its accomplishment, that a portion of land sufficient for the buildings, together with fifty shares on the Potomac River, fast becoming very valuable, had been appropriated by the President of the United States, that there would doubtless be many liberal donations and subscriptions both in this country and in Europe toward its support, and that it would also introduce youths from other countries and tend to the general wealth of this country by the more general dissemination of useful knowledge.

The record adds:

Mr. Madison moved that it be referred to a select committee, and he conceived that it would be proper for the same committee to take up that point of the President's speech which relates to the same subject.

Mr. W. Smith wished to inquire of the gentleman from Virginia, whether it would not be more orderly for the memorial to lie on the table until that part of the President's speech came up under discussion in the House. He suggested this idea from the consideration that it would look more respectful to the Chief Magistrate to let it come from him as he had recommended it to the attention of the House in his address.

Mr. Madison replied that it would be more consistent with order for the memorial to go through a select committee.[2] * * *

The motion passed, and a committee of three members was appointed.

---

[1] Annals, 4th Cong., 2d sess., p. 1591.   [2] Id., pp. 1600, 1601, 1694-7, 1704-11.

XXV. The affirmative action of James Madison on December 21, 1796, and of the committee to whom was referred the said memorial of the commissioners aforesaid, and of which committee he was chairman, in reporting back such memorial together with the following resolution:[1]

*Resolved,* That it is expedient at present that authority should be given, as prayed for by the said memorial, to proper persons to receive and hold in trust pecuniary donations in aid of the appropriations already made towards the establishment of a university within the District of Columbia.[1]

This resolution was made the order of the day for the Monday following, when it was called up and discussed, laid over, and discussed again and again until, on the 27th of December, by a vote of 37 to 36, it was postponed until certain information could be obtained from the legislature of Maryland, and was not again considered.

XXVI. The cordial support by John Adams of the general principles of according aid to progress in science and learning, as shown—

(1) By his part in the establishment of the American Academy of Arts and Sciences, incorporated by the legislature of Massachusetts, in 1780.

(2) By his support of the propositions of Madison and Pickering to put a provision for a national university into the Constitution of the United States. (See No. IV.)

(3) By the spirit of his inaugural address of March 4, 1797, referring as it did with usual warmth to his—

Love of science and letters and a wish to patronize every rational effort to encourage schools, colleges, and universities, academies, and every institution for propagating knowledge, virtue, and religion among all classes of the people, not only for the benign influence on the happiness of life in all its stages and classes, and of society in all its forms, but as the only means of preserving our Constitution from its natural enemies, the spirit of sophistry, the spirit of party, the spirit of intrigue, the profligacy of corruption, and the pestilence of foreign influence.[2]

(4) By the warm hospitality he is known to have extended to the subject of a national university whenever introduced.

That he did not directly and explicitly recommend the establishment of such an institution was manifestly because he deemed the time and circumstances unpropitious and did not wish to make a fruitless attempt.

XXVII. Washington's last will and testament, July 9, 1799:

It has always been a source of serious regret with me to see the youth of these United States sent to foreign countries for the purpose of education, often before their minds were formed, or they had imbibed any adequate ideas of the happiness of their own; contracting too frequently principles unfriendly to republican government, and to the true and genuine liberties of mankind; which, thereafter, are rarely overcome. For these reasons it has been my ardent wish to see a plan devised on a liberal scale, which would have a tendency to spread systematic ideas through all the parts of this rising empire, thereby to do away local attachments and State prej-

[1] American State Papers, No. 91.  [2] Annals, 4th Cong., 2d sess., p. 1585.

udices, so far as the nature of things would, or indeed ought to, admit, from our national councils.  Looking anxiously forward to the accomplishment of so desirable an object as this is (in my estimation), my mind has not been able to contemplate any plan more likely to effect the measure, than the establishment of a university in a central part of the United States, to which the youths of fortune and talents from all parts thereof might be sent for the completion of their education in all the branches of polite literature; in arts and sciences, in acquiring knowledge in the principles of politics and good government, and (as a matter of infinite importance, in my judgment) by associating with each other, and forming friendships in juvenile years, be enabled to free themselves in a proper degree from those local prejudices and habitual jealousies which have just been mentioned, and which, when carried to excess, are never failing sources of disquietude to the public mind, and pregnant of mischievous consequences to this country: under these impressions, so fully dilated,   *   *   *

I give and bequeath in perpetuity the fifty shares (value, $500 each) which I hold in the Potomac Company (under the aforesaid acts of the legislature of Virginia) toward the endowment of a university to be established in the District of Columbia under the auspices of the General Government, if that Government should incline to extend a fostering hand toward it; and until such a seminary is established and the funds arising on these shares shall be required for its support, my further desire is that the profit accruing therefrom shall, whenever dividends are made, be laid out in purchasing stock in the Bank of Columbia, or some other bank at the discretion of my executors, or by the Treasurer of the United States for the time being, under the direction of Congress; and the dividends proceeding from the purchase of such stock is to be invested in more stock, and so on until a sum adequate to the accomplishment of this object is obtained.[1]

Would it not be a very proper thing for the Congress of the United States, as the fiduciary of so sacred a trust, to institute without further delay an inquiry into the whole subject of what has become of the property interests thus committed to its keeping?  And in case it should be found impracticable to recover what has thus been lost through neglect, could the Government justly do less than to make it good, both the principal and the compound interest enjoined, by according such aggregate sum as a part of what will be required as a foundation for the university so wisely planned by Washington?

XXVIII. The memorial of Samuel Blodget, presented to the Congress of the United States Monday, January 10, 1803, as published by himself in Economica:

Mr. Van Ness presented a representation from Samuel Blodget on the subject of a national university, as follows:

The memorial of Samuel Blodget, late supervisor of the city of Washington, represents, that owing his appointment chiefly to his zeal in forming several probationary plans for a national university, he conceived it an indispensable duty, after the death of Washington, to follow the commanding advice and noble example of the common father of his country, so irresistibly portrayed in his farewell address, and in the clause of his will annexed to his liberal donation therefor.  In thus calling, most respectfully, the attention of your honorable body to this part of the will of Washington, he fulfills a promise made in behalf of more than one thousand subscribers to the same object, whose respectable names accompany this memorial, with

[1] Sparks, i, 572.

a request that a committee may be appointed to consider what portion of the public lots, and of lands in the western territory of the United States, shall be appropriated by Congress to this important institution, in addition to the contents of either of the sites already contemplated therefor within the city of Washington, by Washington himself, and by the commissioners thereof. And further, to consider the expediency (should it comport with the monumental plan to be adopted) of erecting the statue of 1783, or, in lieu thereof, any appropriate and characteristic equestrian statue of the original founder of the national university, as a beautiful centerpiece for the entire plan, to be surrounded by halls and colleges as they may be built in succession by the fund to which the whole people of America are now so liberally and honorably contributing by voluntary subscriptions from Maine to Georgia, inclusive, thus virtually following an ancient custom of the original Americans, when men, women, and children all carried a stone to the monumental pile of a beloved chief.

It is humbly conceived that no further aid will be necessary for your honorable body to give till in your wisdom it may be deemed proper to follow the sublime and prophetic advice of Washington, and to assume the entire direction of the most important object ever contemplated in the united efforts of all parties, persuasions, and classes of the American people, under a firm belief that the governmental plan and synopsis thereof will be maturely considered and wisely adapted to promote the views of the sage and provident Washington, namely, "to do away with local attachments and State prejudices, as far as the nature of things would or indeed ought to admit, from our national councils;" and, in short, to promote a true *amor patriæ*, as well as the advancement of new arts and universal science, in all useful knowledge, while "our youth, by associating with each other for these purposes, and forming friendships in their juvenile years, will free themselves from those narrow local prejudices which, when carried to excess, are never-failing sources of disquiet to the public mind and pregnant of the most mischievous consequences to this country."

Such are the principles under which this sublime institution, founded by Washington, and indubitably the best monument to his memory, is now rapidly progressing, to the immortal honor of the American name; nor does it require uncommon inspiration to foretell, that so long as it shall continue true that parents are naturally attached to the most amiable of their offspring, so long will the founders throughout the Union, themselves and their posterity, delight to preserve a noble fabric, which in itself will unite the most sublime points that can with reason interest a generous, industrious, and an enlightened people, and equally endear them to their country and to each other. And so long as the divine principles that gave birth and strength to the infancy of the university may continue, so long by turning the tide of emigration in search of learning shall the American character be the pride and boast of the liberal and learned of all nations and the dread of every foe to human excellence.

A synopsis for the university, uniting with it a plan for a free college, adopting and combining therewith the interest of the existing seminaries throughout the Union, accompany this memorial, together with descriptions or duplicates of several monumental plans, which will remain before the present committee of subscribers till Congress may think proper to assume the entire direction of this object, in conformity with the ardent wishes and earnest advice so irresistibly enforced by Washington.[1]

XXIX. The memorial of Samuel Blodget, presented to the House of Representatives on December 23, 1805, and thus referred to in the annals of Congress:

A memorial was received from Samuel Blodget, representing that subscriptions for a university at Washington have already been made to the number of eighteen thousand and a sum received amounting to $30,000, and requesting Congress to designate the site, with the lots or lands that may be intended therefor, and to grant such further patronage as they may think proper. [1]

Reference of the memorial was made to a select committee of five, whose report appears not to have been submitted.

XXX. The earnest efforts of Minister John Barlow for the founding, by Congress, of a great university, as shown—

(1) By his letters to President Jefferson and others, while representing our country at the court of France.

(2) By his " Prospectus of a National Institution to be established in the United States," which opens with these words:

The project for erecting a university at the seat of the Federal Government is brought forward at a happy moment and on liberal principles. We may therefore reasonably hope for an extensive endowment from the munificence of individuals as well as from Government itself. This expectation will naturally lead us to enlarge our ideas on the subject, and to give a greater scope to its practical operation than has usually been contemplated in institutions of a similar nature.

Two distinct objects, which in other countries have been kept asunder, may and ought to be united; they are both of great national importance, and by being embraced in the same institution they will aid each other in their acquisition. These are the advancement of knowledge by associations of scientific men and the dissemination of its rudiments by the instruction of youth. * * * The leading principle of uniting these two branches of improvement in one institution, to be extended upon a scale that will render it truly national, requires some development.

We find ourselves in possession of a country so vast as to lead the mind to anticipate a scene of social intercourse and interest unexampled in the experience of mankind. This territory presents and will present such a variety of productions, natural and artificial, such a diversity of connections abroad, and of manners, habits, and propensities at home, as will create a strong tendency to diverge and separate the views of those who shall inhabit the different regions within our limits. It is most essential to the happiness of the people and to the preservation of their republican principles that this tendency to a separation should be overbalanced by superior motives to a harmony of sentiment, that they may habitually feel that community of interest on which their federal system is founded. This desirable object is to be attained, not only by the operations of the Government in its several departments, but by those of literature, sciences, and arts. The liberal sciences are in their nature republican; they delight in reciprocal communion; they cherish fraternal feelings and lead to a freedom of intercourse, combined with the restraints of society, which contribute together to our improvement. [2]

(3) By his preparation of a bill to establish such an institution; which bill was introduced in the Senate by Mr. Logan, of Philadelphia, in 1806, and by him reported to the Senate without amendment.

XXXI. The dedication by Samuel Blodget, in 1806, of the proceeds of his " Economica," the first work on political economy ever published in America, to " the benefit in trust for the free education fund of the university founded by George Washington in his last will and testament." [3]

---

[1] Annals, 9th Congress, 1st session, vol. I, p. 301.

[2] Origin of the National Scientific and Educational Institutions in the United

XXXII. The further advocacy of Samuel Blodget, in "Economica," first published in 1806, and republished in 1810, from which the following passages are taken:[1]

After a second visit to Europe the writer returned in 1791, and informed President Washington of the plans he had attempted, from the best points only of the ancient and modern cities of the old world and adapted to his views, for a federal HEART or CAPITOL for this country. But his views for the university were what he most prized, designed in part at The Hague and completed at Oxford, where he had all the universities of ancient and modern times to guide his pencil. From these he borrowed and rejected agreeably to the opinions of the best informed friends he could meet, in order that no childish bias for his own questionable taste might by any means prevent the final success of *the important object in view.*

Again:

That we shall *soon* have a national university *there is now the greatest reason to hope,* since many gentlemen who had read only of some objectionable institutions in Europe, and *who conceived we should of course imitate them,* are now fully convinced that *they were wholly mistaken;* hence many members of Congress have contributed to augment the fund of Washington, on finding that this national institution was intended both to give additional stability to the Union, and yet to assist in the preservation of the independence of each individual State seminary; and that, instead of interfering with the minor schools, it was to have nothing to do with them; that, instead of controlling and humbling the State colleges, it was to contribute to their independency and to increase their importance, inasmuch as a principal controlling power over the most commanding features of the university might be vested with the principals of the State seminaries.

The injuries complained of by some writers, from the too independent situations, by the too great salaries and too secure hold of their durable places in the permanent officers of Europe, will no doubt be avoided in ours, and everything done to make the university not only an epitome to correspond and harmonize always with the principles of our Government and Union, but highly conducive to the preservation of that freedom and independence possessed by all classes of the people composing our American commonwealth.

And again:

Although our Washington had nothing nearer his heart, after the completion of our independence, than a federal city and a central university, as he felt a diffidence when the question for the republican form for the university arose in his mind, lest it might militate with the prejudices of those who were educated at aristocratical seminaries, and thereby fail from formidable opposition, he nevertheless recommended the attention of Congress, in two instances, to this object, in his speeches while President of the United States.

Referring to Washington's confident expectation that his own wishes and bequest would inspire Congress to action, he further says:

*If no aid from Congress or any other source* had followed this noble *challange* of Washington, his donation, *at compound interest,* would in twelve years have given $50,000, and in twenty-four years $100,000. At this period one of the colleges of the university might have been erected and endowed, and yet a part of the surplus might remain at compound interest for the completion of the whole design.

XXXIII. The efforts of Col. John P. Van Ness, president of the Branch Bank of the United States at Washington, of George Washing-

---

[1] Economica, p. 23; Appendix, pp. III–X.

ton Custis, James Davidson, and many other distinguished citizens of Washington, early in the present century, and especially during the the administration of Jefferson; efforts so earnest and practical that, with the proper coöperation of Congress, they would certainly have resulted in the beginning of the proposed university under auspices that would have insured its success.

In further illustration of these efforts, the following extracts from the writings of Mr. Blodget are offered:

The memorial was accompanied by a plan of the equestrian statue of Washington, surrounded by halls and colleges regularly arranged, the whole to be styled "Washingtonia", or, "The Monument to Washington."

It was also stated in handbills that, in conformity with the nomination and appointment at the first meeting of the subscribers, Samuel Blodget had accepted the office of secretary, and the cashier of the Branch Bank of the United States, James Davidson, esquire, that of general treasurer to the subscribers. * * *

It is left to the discretion of a majority of the trustees, at any of their meetings, to commence one of the buildings on such ground as they may deem proper after consulting the President of the United States, with due deference to his opinion in aid of the views of Washington and of the entire plan of his subscribing followers.

\*        \*        \*        \*        \*        \*        \*

It shall be the duty of the secretary to make known, at discretion, to all the friends of science in Europe and universally, that presents are admitted from any quarter of the globe, either to the museum or library, and that foreigners (although not admitted in the list of contributors to the monumental *pile* in honor of the Father of His Country) may, nevertheless, contribute to the endowment of the university in any way consistent with the liberal and honorable views of an institution at which *the youth of all nations* are to be admitted on equal terms, excepting only in the provision for the free education of indigent youth of genius who intend to remain citizens of the United States. [1]

XXXIV. President Jefferson's correspondence with Albert Gallatin, Secretary of the Treasury, in November, 1806, concerning his draft of the annual message to be delivered in December following, from which it appears that he then had two important projects in mind: First, the establishment and endowment of a national university, and, secondly, an amendment to the Constitution explicitly defining the powers of the Federal Government in matters of education and internal improvements, so as to place both of those great interests beyond the possibility of a question.

It further appears that Mr. Jefferson had framed his message with a view to the very certain establishment of a national university by the Fourth Congress, and the appropriation of money therefor out of the general fund so soon as the condition of the Treasury would warrant it.

The letter of November 14 to Mr. Gallatin dealt with questions of the army, the tax on salt, and the university, his comments on the last-named point being as follows:

3. The University. This proposition will pass the States in all the winter of 1807–'08, and Congress will not meet, and consequently can not act on it, till the winter of 1808–'09. The Florida debt will therefore be paid off before the university can call for anything. [2]

---

[1] Economica, Appendix, pp. XIII, XIV.        [2] Writings of Gallatin, Vol. I, p. 313.

XXXV. The very practical letter of Albert Gallatin, Secretary of the Treasury, to President Jefferson, on November 16, 1806, the same being in answer to Mr. Jefferson's of the 14th, and consisting of suggestions concerning the several points embraced in the forthcoming message to Congress, wherein he dealt with the national university passage, sentence by sentence, in the following critical manner:

University.—"They cannot, then, be applied to the extinguishment of debt, etc."
I would wish that between the words *then* and *be* the following should be inserted: "without a modification assented to by the public creditors"; or that the idea should be inserted in some other way in the paragraph.
It will be consistent with the opinion expressed that the extinguishment, etc., and liberties, etc., are the *most desirable of all objects*, and Congress have now under consideration a plan for the purpose, which I submitted last session, and was postponed because reported too late by the Committee of Ways and Means.

Again, under the head "On Fortifications, etc.", he says:

*The surpluses, indeed, which will arise*, etc. [Quoting Mr. Jefferson]. It may be observed on whatever relates to the connection between these surpluses and the supposed improvements and university, first, that, war excepted, the surpluses will certainly and under any circumstances—even while the debt will be in a course of payment—be, after January 1, 1809, sufficient for any possible improvement. I have no doubt that they will amount to at least two millions a year; and, if no modification in the debt takes place, to nearly five. Second, that it will take at least the two intervening years to obtain an amendment for the laws designating improvements and make the arrangements preparatory to any large expense. Third, that the existing surpluses are at this moment sufficient for any university or national institution.
But the whole of this part of the message rests on the supposition that a long time must elapse before we are ready for any considerable expenditure for improvements, and that we would not be able to meet even that for the university before the time which must elapse in obtaining an amendment.
The general scope of this part of the message seems also to give a preference to the university over general improvements; and it must not be forgotten, apart from any consideration of the relative importance, that the last proposition may probably be popular and that the other will quite certainly be unpopular. * * *
It appears to me, therefore, that the whole of that part from the words "the surpluses indeed," etc., to the words "to which our funds may become equal," should undergo a revisal, introducing in the same the substance of the last paragraph of the ninth page, respecting a donation of lands.[1]
[The message will show that the last recommendation prevailed for the most part. But this fact counts for nothing against the exceeding liberality and farsightedness of Mr. Jefferson, who had planned an appeal for money appropriations; nor indeed against his high courage, for that was in the youth and poverty of the nation, when a million seemed an enormous sum, and the people of the country generally had not only not become accustomed to vast expenditures for education, but had not come to even an appreciation of the priceless value of science and learning.]

XXXVI. The sixth annual message of President Thomas Jefferson, delivered on December 2, 1806, containing these words:

Education is here placed among the articles of public care; not that it would be proposed to take its ordinary branches out of the hands of private enterprise, which

manages so much better all the concerns to which it is equal, but a public institution can alone supply those sciences which, though rarely called for, are yet necessary to complete the circle, all the parts of which contribute to the improvement of
the country, and some of them to its preservation.   *   *   *   The present consideration of a national establishment for education particularly is rendered proper by
this circumstance also, that if Congress, approving the proposition, shall yet think
it more eligible to found it on a donation of lands, they have it now in their power
to endow it with those which will be among the earliest to produce the necessary
income.   This foundation would have the advantage of being independent in war,
which may suspend other improvements by requiring for its own purposes the resources destined for them.[1]

XXXVII. The second annual message of President James Madison,
delivered December 5, 1810, embracing these words:

While it is universally admitted that a well-instructed people alone can be permanently a free people, and while it is evident that the means of diffusing and improving useful knowledge from so small a proportion of the expenditures for national
purposes, I can not presume it to be unreasonable to invite your attention to the advantages of superadding to the means of education provided by the several States
a seminary of learning instituted by the national legislature within the limits of
their exclusive jurisdiction, the expense of which might be defrayed or reimbursed
out of the vacant grounds which have accrued to the nation within these limits.
Such an institution, though local in its legal character, would be universal in its
beneficial effects.

By enlightening the opinions, by expanding the patriotism, and by assimilating
the principles, the interests, and the manners of those who might resort to this temple of science, to be redistributed in due time through every portion of the community, sources of jealousy and prejudice would be diminished, the features of
national character would be multiplied and greater extent given to social harmony.
But above all a well-constituted seminary in the center of the nation is recommended
by the consideration that the additional instruction emanating from it would contribute not less to strengthen the foundations than to adorn the structure of our free
and happy system of government.[2]

XXXVIII. The favorable opinion of the committee of the House of
Representatives, to whom was referred, on December 10, 1810, that part
of the President's message which related to the establishment of a seminary of learning by the national legislature; the report of which committee as presented by Samuel L. Mitchell, chairman, while raising
the questions of authority to appropriate money for that purpose, and
of practicability also in view of the then slender resources clearly available, nevertheless set forth the importance of such an institution:

In obedience to the order of the House the committee has duly considered the important matter referred.   An university or institution for the communication of
knowledge in the various departments of literature and science presents to the mind
at one view subjects of the most pleasing contemplation.

To a free people it would seem that a seminary in which the culture of the heart
and of the understanding should be the chief object would be one of the first guards
of their privileges and a leading object of their care.

Under this conviction the patriotic spirit of Washington led him more than once
to recommend in his speeches to Congress such an undertaking.   He even be-

[1] Annals, 9th Cong., 2d sess., p. 14.        [2] Annals, 11th Cong., 3d sess., p. 14.

queathed a legacy to the national university, which he persuaded himself would at some future day be brought into being. Two other Presidents have subsequently presented the subject to the Legislature as worthy of special consideration.

Authorities so respectable in favor of a project so desirable carry great weight.

A central school at the seat of the General Government, darting its rays of intellectual light or rolling the flood of useful information throughout the land, could not fail to make a strong impression. A noble and enlarged institution may be conceived to impart to its pupils the most excellent instruction, and, by properly qualifying persons to be teachers and professors, to introduce an uniform system of education among the citizens. * * *

The Constitution does not warrant the creation of such a corporation by any express provision. But * * * under the right to legislate exclusively over the District wherein the United States have fixed their seat of government Congress may erect a university at any place within the 10 miles square ceded by Maryland and Virginia. This can not be doubted. * * *

The message before the committee proposes, however, the institution of a seminary of learning by the national legislature within the limits of their exclusive jurisdiction, the expense of which may be defrayed or reimbursed out of the vacant grounds which have accrued to the nation within these limits. On inquiry into the value of those public lots they fall so far short of the sum requisite for the object that if there was no constitutional impediment, they could not be relied upon on account of the smallness and unproductiveness of the capital they embrace.[1]

XXXIX. President Madison's seventh annual message, delivered December 15, 1815, wherein he said:

The present is a favorable season, also, for bringing into view the establishment of a national seminary of learning within the District of Columbia, and with means drawn from the property therein, subject to the authority of the General Government. Such an institution claims the patronage of Congress as a monument of that solicitude for the advancement of knowledge without which the blessings of liberty can not be fully enjoyed or long preserved; as a model of instruction in the formation of other seminaries; as a nursery of enlightened preceptors; as a central resort of youth and genius from every part of their country, diffusing on their return examples of those national feelings, those liberal sentiments, and those congenial manners which contribute cement to our Union and strength to the political fabric of which that is the foundation.[2]

XL. President Madison's last annual message, December 3, 1816:

The importance which I have attached to the establishment of a university within this District on a scale and for objects worthy of the American nation, induces me to renew my recommendation of it to the favorable consideration of Congress, and I particularly invite again their attention to the expediency of exercising their existing powers, and where necessary of resorting to the prescribed mode of enlarging them, in order to effectuate a common system of roads and canals, such as will have the effect of drawing more closely together every part of our country by promoting intercourse and improvements and by increasing the share of every part in the common stock of national prosperity.[3]

XLI. Report to the House of Representatives, submitted by Mr. R. H. Wilde in behalf of the committee to whom was referred so much of the President's message as relates to the subject of a national uni-

[1] Ex. Docs., 11th Cong., 3d sess., p. 975.
[2] Annals 14th Cong., 1st sess., p. 17.

versity. Read December 11, 1816, and, with an accompanying bill for the establishment of a national university, referred to a Committee of the Whole House on December 12; which report, with accompanying estimates, is as follows:

The committee of the House of Representatives, to whom was referred so much of the President's message as relates to the subject of a national university, report to the House, as the result of their deliberations, a bill for the erection and endowment of such an institution.

The committee, pursuant to usual forms might, perhaps, without impropriety, regard this a sufficient performance of their duty, and after presenting the bill without comment, have left it to find its appropriate place among others, and to receive or be denied consideration, according to the opinion entertained of its consequence and urgency.

But the number of communications relative to the subject which, though they have received attention, seem to have escaped it because they have not been definitely acted on, may possibly expose the House to a censure more serious than that of merely neglecting the successive recommendations of several successive chief magistrates—a censure as injurious as unjust, yet not unbecoming that body to prevent by making as soon as possible some disposition of a question that ought to be determined on account of its frequent occurrence, even though it should not otherwise be thought particularly interesting. * * *

Your committee therefore have ventured to suggest some of the reasons which recommend the present as a favorable time for investigating, and perhaps, also, adopting, the plan they have proposed.

Among these, the prosperous state of our finances, leaving a large unappropriated surplus, the probability of a long continued peace, the flourishing condition of our Capital, and the facility with which a portion of the public property within it might now be advantageously disposed of, so as at once to increase the convenience of the city and support the proposed institution, may fairly be enumerated.

Besides, the information heretofore collected has enabled the committee to report at an early period, and it is believed that the present session, though inevitably a short one, will not present so many objects of great difficulty or deep interest as entirely to exclude others of a more tranquil and less obtrusive character to which it is possible a portion of time might be profitably devoted.

The acquisition of a scientific and literary reputation not unworthy of their naval and military renown can never be beneath the ambition of a people, since the most durable of all glory is that of exalted intellect. The world is still a willing captive to the spells of ancient genius, and the rivalry of modern empires will be perpetuated by their arts and their learning—the preservers of that fame which arms alone may indeed win, but can never keep.

Any measure which contributes, however scantily, to give American literature and science a rank and name among mankind, can not, therefore, be regarded with indifference by our citizens, and every effort toward that end must be witnessed at the present moment with universal satisfaction, since it will present the interesting spectacle of a young nation bending its whole strength to the pursuit of true greatness, and anxious to emulate all that is amiable in peace as well as all that is noble in war.

That the institution contemplated will have a happy influence on the harmony and welfare of our country and the unity of our national character has been often supposed, and your committee feel inclined to anticipate effects no less happy from its operation on the genius of our people. If America's invention, unassisted as it has been, already excites the astonishment of Europe, what may not be expected from it when aided and encouraged? And why should not aid and encouragement be yielded by institutions like the present, founded and endowed by the munificence of the State?

In our own day we have seen them work wonders in physical science, even when directed by a stern, jealous, and exacting government, which, while training the mind to be quick, dextrous, and daring, darkened its vision and circumscribed its flight. Is it here alone they would be impotent, where no depth could be hidden from its glance, no height forbidden to its wing.

But your committee, fearful of exhausting your patience, forbear to extend this report by arguments which it is easier to multiply than to withhold. For the same reason they refrain from answering objections which could be stated without injury; since in replying to them, force and perspicuity must be sacrificed to conciseness. Nor can such a course be required, when it is intended merely to present a general result, not the particular process of reasoning by which that result has been attained. Your committee, however, desire it to be understood that they have not declined examining any objection which occurred to them; and though some have been found, which, it must be confessed, are not without difficulty, all are thought capable of a satisfactory answer.

Under a conviction, therefore, that the means are ample, the end desirable, the object fairly within the legislative powers of Congress, and the time a favorable one, your committee recommend the establishment of a national university, and have directed their chairman to submit a bill and estimates for that purpose.

*Estimates of the value of lots and squares belonging to the United States, as furnished by communications from the superintendent of the city.*

Four thousand building lots of 5,265 square feet each, and about 2,000-foot front on the waters of the Potomac River, Eastern Branch, valued at.... $750,000
Squares 1 to 6 proposed to be laid off into building lots, containing in the whole, 816,000 square feet, or 155 standard lots, valued at................ 200,000
But the latter amount is the only one which it is supposed could be speedily utilized.
Estimate of the expense of buildings for the national university, on a plan susceptible of extension, but calculated for the present to answer for 160 persons ................................................................. 200,000

Mr. Wilde's committee also presented a bill for the establishment of a National University, as follows:

*Be it enacted, etc.*, That the President of the United States be, and he is hereby, authorized and required to cause to be surveyed and laid off into building lots such part as he shall think proper of the ground reserved of the United States in the city of Washington, and to cause the same to be sold at such times and places and in such proportions and under such regulations as he shall prescribe; and the proceeds thereof, after defraying the charges of survey and sale, to be invested in such stocks or public securities as shall by him be deemed advisable; and the same, when so invested, and the dividends thereon arising, shall constitute a fund for the support of a national university.

SEC. 2. *And be it further enacted*, That the President of the United States be, and he is hereby, authorized to cause to be erected, on such site within the District of Columbia as he shall elect, the buildings necessary for a national university; and for defraying the expense thereof the sum of ——— dollars is hereby appropriated, to be paid out of any money in the Treasury of the United States not otherwise appropriated by law.

SEC. 3. *And be it further enacted,* That the President of the United States be, and he is hereby, required to cause to be prepared and laid before Congress at its next session, a plan for the regulation and government of the said university.[1]

[1] Annals, 14th Cong., 2d sess., p. 257.

Which bill was twice read and committed.

Near the close of the session Mr. Wilde, chairman of the committee, having failed to secure proper consideration for the measure, himself moved and secured its indefinite postponement.

XLII. Support of the general proposition by the Hon. Charles H. Atherton, of New Hampshire, who, seeing that there were doubts in the minds of some as to the powers of Congress under the Constitution, on the 12th of December, 1816, offered for consideration a resolution providing for an amendment thereto, in the following words:

The Congress shall have power to establish a national university.[1]

The House, deeming such amendment unnecessary, decided against the consideration of the resolution by a vote of 86 to 54.

XLIII. The efforts of Drs. Josiah Meigs, Edward Cutbush, Thomas Sewall, Thomas Law, Dr. Alexander McWilliams, and of Judge William Cranch, who, having lost confidence in aid from Congress, avowedly went to work to realize the aspirations of Washington and his successors by founding, first, the Columbian Institute for the Promotion of Arts and Sciences in 1819, and, secondly, the Columbian College, at length incorporated in 1821.

XLIV. The introduction by Mr. Mark L. Hill, of Massachusetts, of the following resolution in the House of Representatives, on the 23d of December, 1819:

Resolved, That a committee be appointed to inquire into the expediency of establishing a National University within the District of Columbia, and that the committee have leave to report by bill or otherwise.[2]

Mr. Hill said, in introducing his motion, that the adoption of this measure had been recommended by each of our illustrious presidents, and with the particular view among other things, to perpetuate the Union and form a national character. Whatever had this tendency he wanted to promote. The motion failed.

XLV. The efforts of President Monroe, whose sympathy with the plans of Washington were often expressed, and who was glad to believe that Columbian College would in time become a national university, as appears from his letter of March 28, 1820, in which he says:

The establishment of the institution within the Federal district, in the presence of Congress and of all the departments of the Government, will secure to those who may be educated in it many important advantages, among which are the opportunity to hear the debates in Congress and in the Supreme Court. * * * If it receives hereafter the proper encouragement, it can not fail to be eminently useful to the nation.

XLVI. The action of Congress in this general interest—

(1) By granting to the Columbian Institute the use of rooms in the

---

[1] Annals, 14th Cong., 2nd sess., p. 268.    [2] Annals, 16th Cong., 1st sess., p. 780.

Capitol, as well as the use of the Hall of Representatives for the annual meetings.

(2) By giving grounds to said institute for a botanical garden, in 1823.[1]

XLVII. John Quincy Adams's no less persistent than brilliant championship of science and learning as demanding the encouragement of Congress, and the strong moral support given by him to the National University in both messages and speeches; as, for example, in his first message, 1825 which contains this eloquent and touching reference to the efforts of Washington in that behalf:

Among the first, perhaps the very first, instruments for the improvement of the condition of men is knowledge; and to the acquisition of much of the knowledge adapted to the wants, the comforts, and enjoyments of human life, public institutions and seminaries of learning are useful. So convinced of this was the first of my predecessors in this office, now first in the memory, as he was first in the hearts, of his countrymen, that once and again, in his addresses to the Congresses with whom he coöperated in the public service, he earnestly recommended the establishment of seminaries of learning, to prepare for all the emergencies of peace and war, a national university, and a military academy. With respect to the latter, had he lived to the present day, in turning his eyes to the institution at West Point he would have enjoyed the gratification of his most earnest wishes. But in surveying the city which has been honored with his name he would have seen the spot of earth which he had destined and bequeathed to the use and benefit of his country as the site for a university still bare and barren.[2]

XLVIII. The action of the United States Senate on Thursday, December 20, 1825, in passing the following resolution, upon motion of Mr. Robbins, of Rhode Island, namely:

Resolved, That so much of the President's message as relates to a National University be referred to a select committee to consist of —— members, that said committee be instructed to report upon the expediency of such an institution, and if deemed by them expedient, to report the principles on which it ought to be established and a plan of organization that will embody those principles.[3]

XLIX. The efforts, in 1820 to 1827, of the eloquent Dr. Horace Holley, D. D., president of Transylvania University, Kentucky, whose views and earnest advocacy of them were made the subject of eulogy by his biographer.

L. The no less zealous efforts of Dr. Charles Caldwell, professor in Transylvania University, especially by means of his biography of Dr. Holley, published in 1828, in which he says of him:

For the better and more certain accomplishment of this latter purpose [to promote progressiveness in education and uniformity throughout the country], he was an advocate for the erection of a national university and the arrangement of schools on a federal plan, analogous to that of our political institutions. He was an advocate, indeed, for the federalizing of everything susceptible of such modification, with a

---

[1] Annals, 18th Cong., 1st sess., p. 787.
[2] Cong. Debates, vol. II, part 2, 19th Cong., 1st sess., Appendix, p. 6.

view to the production and confirmation of federal feelings, practices, and habits, to strengthen throughout the country the federal and national bond and aid in perpetuating the union of the States. For he believed that as concerns the permanency of that union, the stability and endurance of a moral tie, the result of education, social intercourse, early friendships formed at school by leading characters, and a consistent interchange of kind offices, the whole cemented and strengthened by a liberalizing and humanizing spirit of letters derived from a central and common source, are much more to be relied on than those of a connection exclusively political.

As a further reason for advocating the establishment of a national university, he believed that in the nature of things great literary institutions are best calculated for the production of great men, at least of accomplished scholars and pupils distinguished for attainments in science. For, morally and intellectually, as well as physically, it is the law of creation that everything begets in its own likeness. * * * A national university, therefore, being necessarily a grand and magnificent institution, on the same scale must be the educated men it would regularly send forth to participate in the management of national affairs and shed a luster on their native country.

His views of the important influence of a great national institution did not stop here. Considering it as operating on a much more extended scale and covering a field of wider compass, he duly appreciated the effects it would produce on our literary and scientific reputation as a people, in foreign countries. He believed that it would tend much more certainly and effectually than any other measure to secure to us, in that species of reputation, the same ascendency which we are hastening to acquire in arts and arms, and which we have already acquired in practical legislation and diplomatic policy.

LI. The action of Congress in appropriating $25,000 cash to Columbian College, with the approval of President Jackson, in 1832, and that, too, on account of the generally acknowledged "utility of a central literary establishment", and of the failure hitherto to make any more distinct recognition of the recommendations of Washington and of other Presidents.[1]

---

It should be said in this connection that during the years between 1849 and the opening of the late civil war there was a temporary revival of the old demand for a national university. The pressing need of such an institution was a common theme of conversation among the leading educators, scholars, and scientists of the time. It found advocacy upon the rostrum and in the public prints. Members of various organizations made it the subject of public discourses, and at one time, as will hereafter appear, something was done toward founding a national university at Albany, New York.

That its advocates did not press the thought of a national university at Washington was, perhaps, because at that time Washington was little more than a mere political center, and a not very attractive one at that, and because sectionalism held such despotic sway as to preclude the thought of governmental action in that behalf. But since they who originated and coöperated in the movement earnestly contended for the main idea of a true university that should be national in character and influence, and since, moreover, nearly, if not literally, all of them twenty

---

[1] Register Debates in Cong., Vol 8, part 3, p. 3210.

years later fully accepted and indorsed the proposition of a national institution to be established in the national capital, with a sufficient endowment secured to it by Congress, it seems proper that place should be accorded to them in this paper.

The subject appears to have been first publicly broached at Albany by Henry J. Raymond, in the State legislature of 1849. Finally, by agreement between leading educators, scholars, scientists, and statesmen, in the year 1851 a preliminary arrangement was made for the organization of a university of the highest type, as the same was then apprehended, and in accordance with the following governing principles:

The concentration of the ablest possible teaching force for each and all the departments of human learning.

The utmost freedom of students to pursue any preferred branch or branches of study.

Support by the State, for a period of two years, of one student from each assembly district, to be chosen by means of open competitive examinations, so conducted by competent examiners as to exclude all considerations but that of real merit; such public support to be had, however, only after at least fifteen departments had been so endowed as to command the best professional talent the country could afford.

The movement awakened so much interest among distinguished educators that conditional engagements are said to have been made with such men as Profs. Agassiz, Peirce, Guyot, Hall, Mitchell, and Dana.

The efforts in this behalf first resulted in the passage on April 17, 1851, of an act to incorporate the "University of Albany." Some forty-eight persons of that city were named as trustees, with power to create departments of medicine and law, and such others as might be deemed desirable. The institution was authorized to confer degrees and was made subject to the visitation of the regents. In accordance with the general plan, on April 21, 1851, a law school was organized, with Thomas W. Olcott, president of the board of trustees; Hon. Greene C. Bronson, president of the faculty, and Ira Harris, Amasa J. Parker, and Amos Dean as the other members. The first course of lectures was begun in the following December by Amos Dean. By a donation of land and by generous contributions from the faculty and private citizens, an excellent building, with considerable equipment, was in time erected. In 1873, upon the establisheent of Union University, the Albany Law School was merged in that institution.

Likewise an attempt was made in 1851 to establish a department of scientific agriculture, and lectures were announced upon geology, entomology, chemistry, and practical agriculture. A course on the "connection of science and agriculture" was begun in January, 1852, by Prof. John F. Norton, of Yale College, at the opening of which, as reported by the Albany Evening Journal, he spoke of the need of a national university as follows:

No one was of more advantage to community than the close, investigating student. He would assuredly bring forth something of value to the world. True science was always useful, always noble, always elevating.  It was thus for the interest of everybody to encourage its advancement.  We had done so but little yet.  Our youth were compelled to cross the Atlantic to find the advantages they wished.  There was no school among us where they could go and find all they desired.

Subsequently, courses of lectures were also delivered by Prof. James Hall and Dr. Goodly.

In March, 1852, there was great activity at Albany among the friends of the proposed national university.  Public meetings were held on the 10th, 11th, and 12th in the Assembly Hall, attended by members of the legislature and addressed by distinguished gentlemen from different parts of the country, including Messrs. Hooper C. Van Vorst, H. J. Hastings, Isaac Edwards, Judge Harris, and Samuel B. Ruggles, Profs. William F. Phelps and Joseph Henry, and Bishop Alonzo Potter.  In order that the sentiments, purposes, and hopes cherished by leading citizens at that time may appear, extracts from the Journal's reports of some of the speeches then made, especially those of March 11, are here introduced.

From the speech of Rev. Dr. Kennedy:

Now, there is an intellectual Mont Blanc as well as a physical, and there are multitudes of young men panting to ascend this mount.  They come from every quarter of our country.  *  *  *  Where are they to find intellectual guides? *  *  *  But further, the character of our political institutions demands that we should have greater facilities for education.  These institutions rest upon the fundamental principle that all men are born equal.  This is a great practical principle with us, for we have no aristocracy here.  *  *  *  The road to eminence must be opened to the masses—equally open to all.  There are no royal avenues; intellect must be the recommendation.  *  *  *  We should encourage the desire and furnish the means by which to gratify the aspirations of those who wish to be master in whatever pursuit or calling they engage.

There is another demand for such an institution.  It seemed to him that there was a native energy in the American mind and character that asked for means for greater development than has been furnished.  As a nation we are in our infancy; we have accomplished much; not by the means at hand, but by the energy we possess—by indomitable perseverance.  *  *  *  American ingenuity and energy have done much and will yet do more.  Let, then, this energy and genius be fostered.  Give them facilities for improvement and you will see yet greater wonders.

Prof. O. M. Mitchell, director of the Cincinnati Observatory:

The question had been asked, was such a university needed?  *  *  *  He thought it not requisite to argue this point, but would take it for granted that a necessity exists.  He had about him a sort of devotion to his own country.  He could not consent in his humble way to follow eternally the lead of others.  Europe has pointed to us and said, "Behold, a nation of money-getters!  They understand how to gather the money and they hold it in a firm grasp."  They say, "Where are your La Places, your Newtons, your Miltons, your Shakespeares?"

Alas, we have not been able to answer these inquiries in a way to gratify our national ambition.  *  *  *

It was not contemplated to take young men whose minds are not trained, but after they have been trained, it is to open up to them a grand field of inquiry.  He referred to the great benefits conferred by European universities.  There it was that you find concentrated everything that is truly glorious in science, emanating from the great emporium of knowledge.

## From the address of Hon. Samuel B. Ruggles, of New York City:

For what was the theory in regard to public works? Was it not they would lessen not only national but commercial and social inequalities; that they would place the poor by the side of the rich—inferior districts by the side of the superior; the agricultural by the side of the trading communities; and, so far as nature's laws would permit, would equalize the condition of all?

We hold to a similar theory in regard to education, and that it is its true aim and best effect to raise up the low, the helpless, the down-trodden, to lessen the inequalities that prevail in the intellectual culture and condition of the people, to remove or batter down the obstacles that retard the advancement of the sons of poverty and misfortune, and to place them side by side, on equal terms, and in fair and open competition with the favored sons of fortune.

By a similar analogy we hold that in education, as in public works, and in truth in all the great efforts of mankind, the secret of success is found in concentrating strength. * * *

But here, just at this very point, we suddenly encounter a school of political philosophy—not very numerous, for, God be praised, the race is nearly extinct—whose great delight it is to proclaim aloud that the "world is governed too much", and that government has no right to do more than "*protect a man in the possession of his life, liberty, and property, and must then stop*"! * * *

Now, if this miserable doggerel were true, even to its letter, it would not be difficult to show that the protection of "property" itself would imperiously require ample and extended education as its only means of safety against ignorance, its deadliest enemy. But we descend to no such special pleading. We meet the proposition at once in its full extent and deny that any such limitation of the great blessing of human government, the greatest of all social blessings God has bestowed upon man, has any foundation or justification in experience, reason, or authority. We brand and denounce the whole doctrine as mischievous, cruel, and destructive—the diseased offspring of feeble minds and cankered hearts. * * *

It is, then, this unequaled variety, this unprecedented combination of intellectual strength, which is to impart to the university its distinguishing characteristic. Here the pupil of any taste and aim can select the subject he wishes to pursue, each and all to any extent he may desire.

*      *      *      *      *      *      *

A good example of an institution like that we propose, made for the people and composed of people coming from the people, is furnished by what was once our sister Republic of France. It was among the earliest results of the downfall of the royal power in 1792. The Polytechnic, then called the central school of Paris, was born and baptized in blood and slaughter, amid the most fearful spasms of the revolution; but it contained the one vital, all-important, all-possessing element of pupils collected by fair, free, open competition among the people. * * *

We further contend that no State can afford that any one of its people shall needlessly be deprived of any of his natural powers, or that those powers shall be lost through want of proper culture and development, and that in a merely economic view the State suffers positive pecuniary loss when any useful faculty is thus needlessly neglected or suffered to lie dormant.

It was in this light that the prudent and calculating but sagacious Dutchmen, ancestors of those who founded this goodly city of Albany, in which we are now standing, viewed this matter. It was in Holland—economical, industrious, thrifty, liberty-loving Holland—that learning was most highly valued. It was amid the sunken fens and marshes of the Rhine and the Vecht, holding fearful and unequal conflict with the ocean, that the hardy burghers, who sent forth the Rhinelanders and Van Vechtens to carry the virtues of their parent laws into another hemisphere, founded the cities where science loved to dwell. In the early days of their republic, while battling with the whole power of the Spanish crown, it fell to the arms of the city of Leyden—heroic Leyden—to struggle for her new-born liberty through a siege attended by slaughter and famine and all the superadded sufferings and horrors which cruelty could afflict or courage endure. And what was the magnificent answer of these gallant, far-seeing Dutchmen to their grateful stadtholder when he proffered them exemption from taxation as a reward for their matchless constancy and valor? Like their descendants, they loved their guilders, but they rejected the proffered boon; with a love of letters only exceeded by their love of country, to a man they exclaimed, "Give us a university!" And thus the great university of Leyden came into the world, where for centuries it has stood and still stands, the proudest monument of Dutch courage and Dutch intelligence. From its ancient and honored halls hosts of illustrious men have gone forth to benefit and bless mankind. Need we do more than name Grotius, the jurist, whose exalted equity and transcendent genius, curbing the violence of war, has given law to the nations, or Boerhaave, the physician, whose world-wide fame, spreading far beyond the uttermost limits of Christendom, brought mighty potentates from Asia to acknowledge his consummate, unequaled skill?    *    *    *

My friends, let not such examples be lost.    *    *    *    Heaven has cast our favored lot in the early morning of our national existence; let us in grateful remembrance hand down to our descendants proof of our wise and provident regard in institutions deeply engrafted upon the affections of the people, and which shall brighten and adorn the coming days of our Republic, great and enduring seats of science, where learning and liberty, knowledge and virtue shall flourish side by side with law and order in ever-increasing vigor to the latest moment of time.

Dudley Observatory, the third institution inaugurated as a part of the proposed national university, named after Charles E. Dudley, of Albany, and built and endowed by his widow, was incorporated April 3, 1852. The inaugural address was delivered August 26, 1856, by Edward Everett, during the meeting of the American Association for the Advancement of Science. The institution ere long received contributions to the amount of $150,000. The charge of it was intrusted to Profs. Bache, Henry, Gould, and Peirce. Subsequently Prof. Mitchell was appointed director, and was succeeded by Prof. George W. Hough. The observatory also became afterwards a part of Union University.[1]

Profound interest in the general proposition was also shown by the remarks of eminent citizens at the opening of the fifth session of the American Association for the Advancement of Education, held at New York in 1855.

(1) By Alex. Dallas Bache, Superintendent of the Coast Survey, retiring president:

Allow me now, however, before yielding my place, to say a few words upon the themes which, had opportunity been offered, I would have desired to bring in a more appropriate shape before you. These are, *a great university, the want of our country, in this our time*, and the *common school and college, fragments of systems requiring to be united into one.* The various efforts made to establish a great university within the last thirty years are well known to you.    *    *    *    A great university, in the full organization of its faculties of science and letters, and, if you please, of law, medicine, and theology, is, I am persuaded, the want of our country.    *    *    *

---

[1] Historical and Statistical Record of the University of the State of New York, pp. 173–'7.

The mode of organization of such a university I can not now touch upon, but would merely say a few words in regard to the relations which its faculty of sciences would sustain to education generally and to the progress of science. * * * Such an institution requires a large endowment, not to be expended in costly buildings, but in museums, laboratories, collections of nature and art, and in sustaining liberally a corps of professors worthy of the institution and of the country. * * * If the common school were so organized as to be fit for all, as it is already in some of our cities; if it led to the high school and college, and then to the university, so that our youths who have the time and talent necessary should find an open way from the beginning to the end of the system, these institutions would help, not hinder each other; waste of time, money, and intellect would be avoided, and the youth of our country be truly educated.[1]

### (2) By Rev. Charles Brooks, Massachusetts:

The Anglo-Saxon blood on this side of the globe must faithfully educate and peacefully lead the other races. It is our destiny and *we must fulfill it.* We must, therefore, establish a national system of free and universal culture upon the broadest basis of pure democratic republicanism, and then carry it into effect by the united wisdom and the resistless energy of a rich, powerful, intelligent, and Christian people.

Such a system, suited to our thousand years of future growth and nameless millions of inhabitants, will place us *at the head of the nations,* while it becomes the progressive agency, the conservative power, and the eternal blessing of our national life. * * *

And the natural continuation of this system is the true republican idea of education. Carry out this republican idea, that every child has a right to culture, that every town is bound to see that its children receive education, and it follows that every State is morally and politically bound to develop all the talents that God sends into it, and it is therefore the duty of the State to establish a free college, and thus to carry education still onward and make each child what God designed that he should be. This, I apprehend, is the true republican idea of education. This is the idea which I wish to see established in all the republics of South America; and after all this comes the noble plan which has been so admirably and eloquently described by our retiring president, a university into which the best scholars from our colleges may go and receive from the country such culture of the peculiar talents which each possesses as shall fit him to answer the purpose for which he was born into the world; that he may fill the spot which God ordained that he should fill; that he may work without friction in his own proper place in the world.[2]

### (3) By Prof. Benjamin Peirce, of Cambridge, Massachusetts:

There is one subject spoken of in the address of the retiring president in which, with him, I have taken great interest, and with him have suffered disappointment. It is the establishment of a great university. I can, as he can, speak upon the subject, now at least, with independence. There was a time, when we were engaged in our efforts at Albany, when I should have been willing to embark in such an institution; when, against the entreaties and almost the tears of my family and friends, I should have been willing, for the sake of the cause of education in the country, to have abandoned existing connections with another plan of learning to join that institution. But since that time I have designedly made such engagements as will make it impossible now. I am, therefore, as free as the president to speak upon the subject. It seems to me to have a very close and important connection with the subject referred to by Rev. Mr. Brooks—the duty of the Government to educate every citizen; its duty because, if for no other reason, it is good economy on the part of the State to educate every one of its citizens to the utmost extent; just as good economy as for the farmer to make the most of every portion of his stock. The State will be benefited by educating every man to the highest point that he can be, and it will by the best investment it can make of its funds to invest them in intellect developed to its utmost capacity.

It seems to me that a great university in connection with the colleges and high schools is of the greatest importance, because it gives the only means of adapting education to every variety of intellect.  *  *  *

I know it is a popular doctrine that genius will find its way; but I doubt whether genius will necessarily be developed of itself. We have another popular doctrine which is much nearer to the truth, which is, that opportunity makes the man. We can not have a great man unless he has ability, but neither can we have a great man who has not an opportunity worthy to develop him. It is important, therefore, that in our public provision for education we should afford this opportunity.[1]

The oration of Dr. Benjamin Apthorp Gould, the astronomer, on July 15, 1856, before the Connecticut Beta of the Phi Beta Kappa Fraternity of Trinity College, Hartford, Connecticut, should also be cited:

The purport of my words to-day is this: Shall our zone-bounded realm, lighted by Southern Cross and Northern Crown, shaded by its fir and larch and palm and vine, bearing in its maternal bosom the hope, not of a hemisphere, but of a world; whose presence is a speck in contrast with its awfully portentous future; with a richness of resources and a teeming wealth surpassing that of any other empire on the earth  *  *  *  shall we Americans never aspire to what suffering Leyden craved, what conquered Prussia looked to for regeneration, and without which all the clustered glories of the Rhine lacked their highest charm? No more must the long procession of our youth toil through its weary pilgrimage across the Atlantic wave in search of that mental sustenance which it has the right to demand at the hands of its fatherland.  *  *  *

But it may be asked by some: What means all this clamor for a university when we have already a hundred and twenty-seven in the land, and every year is adding to its numbers?  *  *  *  The reason is very simple. It is not of colleges that we are speaking; it is of a university.  *  *  *

By college I understand the high educational seminary which, if not the most exalted for the students of specialties, is yet the highest for the youth who seek that mental discipline, that classic culture, that literary refinement which must be drawn from the bosom of an alma mater, and of which we say "emollit mores nec sinit esse feros."  *  *  *

By "university," on the other hand, I understand the *universitas litterarum*, the Πανεπιστήμιον, an institution where all the sciences in the complete and rounded extent of their complex whole are cultivated and taught, where every specialty may find its votaries, and may offer all the facilities required by its neophytes. Its aim is not so much to make scholars as to develop scholarship, not so much to teach the passive learner as to educate investigators, and not merely to educate but to spur on.  *  *  *

Surely there can be no confusion as to the boundary line between these two distinct institutions. One is designed to answer the demands of the community and of the age; the other to point out the paths and lead our country on to a high, nobler, holier, sublimer eminence than it could otherwise attain or than would otherwise be striven for.

Centralization is a word and an idea now far from popular. But this, like most other principles, has its good as well as evil consequences. And while we, under democratic and republican institutions, feel the full force of the objections to that political centralization under which we see so many nations of the old world tottering and sinking, we are too apt to overlook the incalculable, the unspeakable advantages which flow from the concentrated accumulation of a whole nation's genius and talent. * * * There is no substitute for the "encounter of the wise." Like · that of flint and steel it strikes out without cessation the glowing sparks of truth; like that of acid and alkali it forms new, unexpected, and priceless combinations; like the multiplication of rods in the fagot, it gives new strength to all while taking it from none. A spiritual stimulus pervades the very atmosphere electrified by the proximity of congregated genius, its unseen but ever active energy—floating in the air, whispering in the breeze, vibrating in the nerves, thrilling in the heart—prompts to new effort and loftier aspiration through every avenue which can give access to the soul of man.

Such centralization is eminently distinguished from political centralization, and by this peculiarity, among others, that far from being a combination for the sake of arguing and exercising a greater collective power, it acts, on the contrary, to augment individual influence. While forming a nucleus for scientific, literary, artistic energy, it is not a gravitation center toward which everything must converge and accumulate, but is an organic center whose highest function is to arouse and animate the circulation of thought and mental effort and profound knowledge. It is a nucleus of vitality rather than a nucleus of aggregation. * * * An intellectual center for a land is a heart, but subject to no induration; it is a brain, but liable to no paralysis; an electric battery which cannot be consumed; it is a sun without eclipse, a fountain that will know no drought. To such a university our colleges would look for succor in their need, for counsel in their doubt, for sympathy in their weal or woe. There is no one of them but would develop to new strength and beauty under its genial emanations; none so highly favored or so great that its resources and powers would not expand; none too lowly to imbibe the vitalizing, animating influences which it would diffuse like perfume.

\* \* \* \* \* \* \*

We want no university keeping up with the times and commending itself to the public approval. We want one which shall be just as far ahead of the age as is consistent with being within hail; which shall enlarge and expand the mind and taste and appreciation of the public, compelling the admiration of the public, not soliciting its approval. We want a university which, instead of complying with the demands of the age, shall create, develop, and satisfy new and unheard-of requisitions and aspirations—which, so far from adapting itself to the community, shall mold that community unto itself, and which through every change and every progress shall still be far in advance of the body social, guiding it, leading it, urging it, drawing it, pulling it, hauling it onward.

\* \* \* \* \* \*

The university will contain a soul, a restless, striving, throbbing, impelling, shaping, creative vitality; and will become, not an Italian, nor a French, nor an English, nor a Spanish, nor a German, but preëminently an American university—glowing with American fire, pulsating with American aspirations, and, strange as the words may sound to us to-day, radiating with what will then be American scholarship, American depth of thought, American thoroughness of research, American loftiness of generalization. * * * It will bring the refining power of ancient lore and classic elegance to balance and counteract the all-pervading tendency to mere material science; it will leaven the tone of thought throughout the world by introducing the precision of exact science where the vagueness and confusion of the school men have long reigned; it will lift the philosophical and philological sciences to a far higher scope and standard as specialties, while it unfetters the struggling mind from the incubus of an antiquity which recognizes no progress, a conservatism which excludes all things which are or ever have been new. For I assure you that there never existed a university which surrendered either to conservatism or radicalism; never a university which was not eminently nationalizing in its tendency. * * * Under the most absolute despotisms the universities have been nurseries of political liberty; under the most intolerant of creeds they have fostered freedom of thought. \* \* \*

Found the American university and throngs of European youth shall crowd its halls, carrying back with them American ideas to ennoble their own lands, bringing hither with them counterpoises of transatlantic thought that shall ennoble ours, and both by their coming and their going cementing the family of nations in bonds of mutual sympathy and attachment; found it, though it cost the whole revenues of a capital. Let earth, air, and sea bring their tribute; let California and India pour in their gold, and the busy marts of men their gains, till this great work is done. Thus shall we achieve the glory of a nation, the welfare of a continent, the advancement of the race, and crown the clustering hopes of humanity with more than full fruition.[1]

The paper contributed by "An Alabamian" (possibly the able president of the University of Alabama) to the American Journal of Education, in 1857, is in the same vein:

\* \* \* That end is the enlistment of the United States of America in the enterprise of founding a great national university. This can only be accomplished through the million. A people is to be enlightened in regard to a thing which they can not comprehend, but which, by possibility, they may be made to apprehend sufficiently to lead to action. What grander labor ever awaited performance? It is to be done, if at all, through the instrumentality of American scholars. They are fully alive to its importance, but they contemplate with aching hearts the difficulty of the task. \* \* \*

Here, then, we may rehearse in brief the three chief reasons why the idea of an American university, so timely and beneficent in its conception and so respectably enunciated to the world, seems to have fallen immediately into oblivion.

1. A want of confidence in the permanency of the Federal Union.

2. A lack of ability on the part of the people to discern the need of such an institution.

3. The inadequacy of the means hitherto employed in its promotion. \* \* \*

We are in pressing need of an American university. We can have one if we will. Let us use the requisite means. We have excellent colleges; let them be sustained We have excellent State universities, (so called); let the States rally to their sup port. But the more these are multiplied and patronized, the louder and more urgent is the demand for a national university.

In order to be national it should be located upon common ground. Under existing circumstances it would be wholly impracticable in New York, or Alabama, or anywhere outside the District of Columbia. The Smithsonian Institution and the National Observatory form a worthy nucleus. If each State should appropriate $200,000 toward an endowment a fund would thus be created of more than six millions, upon the strength of which a very respectable beginning could be made. Its permanent nationality would seem to require that each State be equally represented, both in the fund and in the management. \* \* \*

And it may not be amiss to add that a great Southern university is already spoken of; the establishment of which would defeat forever the project herein considered. It would doubtless be followed (if not preceded) by a great Northern university, and then a great Western university. There would then be three grand centers of attraction and influence, tending rather to destroy than cement the Union. To avert such a consequence, let the plan of an American university be matured without unnecessary delay. Sectional enterprise can not long be held in abeyance. Shall we hear a response from the North?[2]

---

[1] Barnard's Jour. of Education, 1856, pp 273–293.

[2] Jour. of Education, Vol III, p. 215.

LII. The efforts of John W. Hoyt, as United States Commissioner to the Paris Exposition of 1867, whose official report of some
400 pages, submitted to the Secretary of State after a personal inspec-
tion of every university in Europe and America, concludes as follows:

So much is already beyond question, namely, that the university of the future is
to be, not the mere college of America, nor even the college supplemented by one or
more poorly equipped professional schools; not that loose aggregation of grammar
schools, supplemented by a few poorly attended courses of university lectures, that
wear the title by courtesy in England; not the French grouping of academic faculties, limited—especially in the departments of letters and science—to a quite too
narrow field of study; not the university of Spain, or Portugal, or Italy, from whose
faculties for the higher general culture the powers of attraction and inspiration have
long since departed; not the Scandinavian or Slavonian university, cast in the mold
of mediæval times, or at the best a mixture of the old and more modern types; nor
yet the Germanic university, found, with but minor modifications, in all the states
of Germany, in Austria, Switzerland, Holland, and Denmark, and which, though
wherever found it represents the highest existing type, is nevertheless everywhere
too limited in scope and generally too lax in its regulations.

It is to be not any of these, but rather an institution more ample in its endowment,
broader in its scope, more complete in its organization, more philosophical and
practical in its internal regulations, and certainly not less high than the highest in
all its educational standards; an institution above and beyond the best of the gym-
nasia, Latin schools, high schools, academies, and colleges, and, on its own higher
plane, for the extension and diffusion of all branches of knowledge; a broad and noble
institution where the love of all knowledge, and of knowledge as knowledge, shall be
fostered and developed; where all departments of learning shall be equally honored,
and the relations of each to every other shall be understood and taught; where the students devoted to each and all branches of learning, whether science, language, literature, or philosophy, or to any combination of these constituting the numerous
professional courses of instruction, shall intermingle and enjoy friendly intercourse
as peers of the same realm; where the professors, chosen, as in France and Germany,
after trial, from among the ablest and best scholars of the world, possessed of absolute freedom of conscience and of speech, and honored and rewarded more nearly in proportion to merit, shall be, not teachers of the known merely, but also earnest searchers
after the unknown, and capable, by their own genius, enthusiasm, and moral power
of infusing their own lofty ambition into the minds of all who may wait upon their
instruction; a university not barely complying with the demands of the age, but
one that shall create, develop, and satisfy new and unheard-of demands and aspirations; that shall have power to fashion the nation and mold the age unto its own
grander ideal; and which, through every change and every real advance of the world,
shall still be at the front, driving back from their fastnesses the powers of darkness,
opening up new continents of truth to the grand army of progress, and so leading the
nation forward, and helping to elevate the whole human race. Such an institution
would be to the world its first realization of the true idea of a university.[1]

LIII. The efforts of John W. Hoyt, by his address before the National Educational Association, at its annual meeting in Trenton, N. J.,
August 20, 1869, on University Progress, wherein it was urged that
"a true university is the leading want of American education," and
that the association should "neither take rest nor allow rest to the
country" until such an institution had been planted and firmly estab-

---

[1] Exposition Reports, Vol. VI, pp. 397, 398.

lished—"a fit illustration of American freedom and of American aspirations for the progress of the race."

LIV. The action of the National Educational Association at the meeting above mentioned, in unanimously adopting the following resolution, offered by Superintendent Andrew J. Rickoff, of Ohio, namely:

*Resolved,* That, in the opinion of this association, a great American university is a leading want of American education, and that, in order to contribute to the early establishment of such an institution, the president of this association, acting in concert with the president of the National Superintendents' Association, is hereby requested to appoint a committee consisting of one member from each of the States, and of which Dr. J. W. Hoyt, of Wisconsin, shall be chairman, to take the whole matter under consideration, and to make such report thereon at the next annual convention of said association as shall seem to be demanded by the interests of the country.[1]

Also by the appointment, as members of said national committee, of the following persons:

Dr. John W. Hoyt, Madison, Wis., chairman; Hon. N. B. Cloud, Montgomery, Ala.; Hon. Thomas Smith, Little Rock, Ark.; Prof. W. P. Blake, San Francisco, Cal.; Hon. B. G. Northrup, New Haven, Conn.; Prof. L. Coleman, Wilmington, Del.; Hon. T. C. Chase, Tallahassee, Fla.; Hon. Newton Bateman, Springfield, Ill.; Hon. B. C. Hobbs, Indianapolis, Ind.; Hon. S. S. Kissell, Des Moines, Iowa; Hon. P. McVicker, Topeka, Kans.; Hon. Z. T. Smith, Frankfort, Ky.; Hon. T. W. Conway, New Orleans, La.; Hon. Warren Johnson, Augusta, Me.; Hon. M. A. Newell, Baltimore, Md.; Hon. Joseph White, Boston, Mass.; Hon. O. Hosford, Lansing, Mich.; Prof. W. F. Phelps, Winona, Minn.; President Daniel Read, Columbia, Mo.; Prof. J. M. McKinsey, Peru, Nebr.; Hon. A. N. Fisher, Carson City, Nev.; Hon. Thomas Hardy, Concord, N. H.; Hon. C. S. Apgar, Trenton, N. J.; Hon. J. W. Bulkley, Brooklyn, N. Y.; Hon. S. S. Ashley, Raleigh, N. C.; Prof. A. J. Rickoff, Cleveland, Ohio; Rev. Geo. H. Atkinson, Portland, Oregon; Hon. J. P. Wickersham, Harrisburg, Pa.; Hon. T. W. Bicknell, Providence, R. I.; Hon. J. K. Jillson, Charleston, S. C.; Rev. C. T. P. Bancroft, Lookout Mountain, Tenn.; Hon. J. S. Adams, Montpelier, Vt.; Hon. W. H. Ruffin, Richmond, Va.; Prof. Z. Richards, Washington, D. C.

LV. The efforts of Dr. William B. Wedgewood, Thomas C. Connelly, John L. Roberts, William H. Chase, S. S. Baker, A. C. Richard, James M. Fuston, encouraged by many citizens of Washington, including especially Dr. C. C. Cox, Prof. Zalmon Richards, Dr. Tullio de Suzzara-Verdi, and Justice Arthur MacArthur, who, on April 14, 1871, procured a charter for the incorporation of a national university, under which at first a law school and afterwards a medical school were opened, with the expectation of making them permanent departments of the university when it should become an established fact. [Both of these professional schools are still in operation, under lead of Chancellor Arthur MacArthur; but they are without endowment, and are only kept alive by voluntary sacrifices on the part of their faculties.]

LVI. The publication by John W. Hoyt, in 1870, of his work on the Progress of University Education, the same being an enlarge-

---

[1] Proceedings Nat. Ed. Ass'n., 1869, p. 23.

ment of the Address above-mentioned, and embracing: (1) The University of the Past; (2) The University of the Present; and (3) The University of the Future. From the closing pages of this work the following extract is made:

If, now, the conclusions reached upon the several questions involved be correct—and a full and free discussion of them is cordially invited—may we not assume that the university of the future ought to be, and is destined to be, not only a higher but a more comprehensive institution than the highest and most complete of those now in existence—an institution high enough to embrace the utmost limits of actual intellectual achievement and broad enough to include every real profession—an institution fulfilling as has never yet been done its three-fold office of giving the highest instruction in every department and alone conferring the highest degrees therein; of extending the boundaries of human knowledge by means of research and investigation, and of exerting a constantly stimulating influence upon every class of schools of lower grade?

The realization of this high ideal will cost large sums of money. Its foundation must be reckoned by millions, its professors by hundreds, and its means of illustration and experiment be extensive in every department. But the results upon our whole system of education and upon the intellectual progress of the people would be beyond calculation.[1]

LVII. The unanimous adoption by the National Educational Association, at its annual meeting at Cleveland, Ohio, in August, 1870, of the, preliminary report of its committee on a national university, from which report the following passages are quoted:[2]

Notwithstanding the many and various uses heretofore made of the term university, it may be assumed, without fear of successful contradiction, that the leading offices of a true university are these:

(1) To provide the best possible facilities for the highest and most profound culture in every department of learning.

(2) To provide the means of a thorough preparation for all such pursuits in life as, being based upon established scientific and philosophical principles, are entitled to rank as professions.

(3) To exert a stimulating and elevating influence upon every subordinate class and grade of educational institutions by holding up before the multitude of their pupils the standard of the highest scholarship, and by preparing for their administrative and instructional work officers and teachers of a higher grade of qualification than would be otherwise possible.

(4) To enlarge the boundaries of human knowledge, by means of the researches and investigations of its professors and fellows, as well as by the researches and investigations of other advanced minds, encouraged to greater activity and led to greater achievements by the influence of the university example.

In so far as any institution, whatever its name or fame, fails in the fulfilment of this general mission, by so much does it fall short of the standard of a true university.

And, again:

Such a university in America would at once become a power, influential alike in furthering and directing our material development, in elevating the character of the lower educational institutions of the country, and in awakening and sustaining higher conceptions of both individual and national culture, thus helping, by a happy

---

[1] University Progress, p. 79.   [2] Proceedings of Nat. Ed. Ass'n, 1869, pp. 97-100.

combination of our own more than Roman energy and religious faith with the grace and refinement of the Greek civilization, to become a nation fully worthy of the future that awaits the United States.

It would do vastly more than this. It would supply to all lands a most important need of the times—a university placed under the benign influence of free civil and religious institutions, and sublimely dedicated to the diffusion and advancement of knowledge. Students of high aspirations, and even ripe scholars of genius, would eventually flock to its halls from every quarter of the globe, adding to the intellectual wealth of the nation should they remain, or bearing with them scions from the tree of liberty for planting in their native lands. And thus America, already the most marvelous theater of material activities, would early become the world's recognized center of intellectual culture as well as of moral and political power.    *    *    *

When a few years since the men of work asked help of the nation for the endowment of schools for the benefit of agriculture and the mechanic arts the Government, with a liberal hand, gave for this noble object 10,000,000 acres of the public domain, to which the individual States and great-hearted men have added no less liberal means. How much more, then, proportionally, will our statesmen in council and liberal patriots yield for the founding and maintenance of one great central institution, to be established in the interest of every profession and of all classes of schools, of a profound and universal culture, of a more perfect intellectual and social development of the whole body of the nation, in the interest of liberty and universal man!

### Finally:

In the opinion of your committee, the attention of the association has not been called to this subject a moment too soon. The trial of its political institutions through which the American nation has just passed; the manner in which the necessity for education as the only guaranty for the perpetuity of these institutions has just been burned into the national consciousness; the pressing demand made by our material and social condition for the best educational facilities the world can furnish, and the fast accumulating evidence that America is surely destined to a glorious leadership in the grand march of the nations—all these constitute an appeal to action which it were criminal to disregard. The necessity is great. The country and the times are ripe for the undertaking.

LVIII. The address of Gen. John Eaton, jr., National Commissioner of Education, before the National Teacher's Association, at Cleveland, August 19, 1870, wherein he said:

Next, as regards the District of Columbia. Here especially in the city of Washington, there should be a model system of education and scientific training for our youth, complete in its buildings, apparatus, and grounds, and in its opportunities for research in letters, science, and art. Where else than at the seat of Government could there more fitly be the crowning university of the land, where every qualified youth could freely pursue any branch of study or experiment desired. The Republic of Switzerland has already set us the example in its federal university. Thus would be realized the ideal dream of the Father of his Country.[1]

LIX. The action of the National Educational Association, at its annual meeting of 1871, held at St. Louis—

(1) In unanimously adopting the second report of the aforesaid committee on a national university; which report, among other things, contained the following:

Your committee are also gratified to be able to report a general concurrence, on the part of the many eminent men who have expressed their views upon the subject, in those large and liberal ideas of university education which only are adequate to the growing and already pressing demands of our country and times.

It was not deemed important in submitting our first report, nor is it necessary in this, to mark the details of what the institution should be. * * * It may be proper, however, to state in general terms:

(1) That it should be broad enough to embrace every department of science, literature, and the arts, and every real profession.

(2) That it should be high enough to supplement the highest existing institutions of the country, and to embrace within its field of instruction the utmost limits of human knowledge.

(3) That, in the interest of truth and justice, it should guarantee equal privileges to all duly qualified applicants for admission to the courses of instruction, and equal rights, as well as the largest freedom, to all earnest investigators in that vast domain which lies outside the limits of acknowledged science.

(4) That it should be so constituted and established as to command the hearty support of the American people, regardless of section, party, or creed.

(5) That its material resources should be vast enough to enable it not only to furnish, and that either freely or at nominal cost, the best instruction the world can afford, but also to provide the best known facilities for the work of scientific investigation, together with endowed fellowships and honorary fellowships, open respectively to the most meritorious graduates and to such investigators, whether native or foreign, as, being candidates therefor, shall have distinguished themselves most in the advancement of knowledge.

(6) That it should be so coördinated in plan with the other institutions of the country as not only in no way to conflict with them, but on the contrary, to become at once a potent agency for their improvement and the means of creating a complete, harmonious, and efficient system of American education. * * *

The idea of a national university, then, is as old as the nation, has had the fullest sanction of the wisest and best men of succeeding generations, and is in perfect harmony with the policy and practice of the Government.[1]

(2) The action of the National Educational Association, at the aforesaid St. Louis meeting of 1871, in creating, as proposed by its said national university committee, a new and permanent committee, "to be charged with the duty of further conducting the enterprise to a successful issue, whether by means of conferences and correspondence, or through the agency of a special convention;" the said permanent committee thus created being constituted as follows, to wit:

Dr. John W. Hoyt, of Wisconsin, chairman; ex-President Thomas Hill, Massachusetts; Mr. E. L. Godkin, New York; Hon. W. P. Wickersham, State superintendent of public instruction, Pennsylvania; Dr. Barnas Sears, Virginia; Col. D. F. Boyd, president University of Louisiana, Louisiana; Dr. Daniel Read, president University of Missouri, Missouri; Dr. W. F. Phelps, president State Normal School, Winona, Minn.; ex-Governor A. C. Gibbs, Oregon; Hon. Newton Bateman, State superintendent of public instruction, Illinois; with the following *ex officio* members: The president of the National Educational Association; the National Commissioner of Education; the president of the National Academy of Sciences; the president of the National Association for the Advancement of Science, and the president of the American Social Science Association.[2]

LX. The preparation, by the aforesaid permanent committee on a national university, in January, 1872, of a bill to be offered to Con-

---

[1] Proceedings Nat. Ed. Assn., 1870, pp. 97–100.　　[2] Id., 1871, pp. 37–41.

gress, and in sending the same to leading citizens in all parts of the country, accompanied by the following request:

DEAR SIR: This draft of a bill to incorporate a national university is merely tentative, and is respectfully submitted to you for criticisms and suggestions, which please forward to the undersigned * * * as early as practicable.

LXI. The valuable assistance of Senator Charles Sumner, who gave much time to this subject, especially in 1872–'73, who aided in maturing the bill of the National Educational Association, and whose interest was so great that he seriously talked of making a systematic effort to secure the founding of the proposed university as the closing labor of his life.

LXII. The preparation, by Dr. O. W. Wight, of a bill to establish a national university for the purpose of elevating the standard of education in the Republic and promoting the intellectual welfare of the people, and the introduction of said bill (S. 859) on March 25, 1872, by Senator Timothy O. Howe.

LXIII. The coöperation of Senators J. W. Patterson, Timothy O. Howe, Mathew H. Carpenter, John J. Ingalls, W. B. Allison, L. Q. C. Lamar, and James H. Garland, Professors Joseph Henry, Spencer F. Baird, and Louis Agassiz, and others, with the National University Committee, in the preparation of the bill finally introduced in both Houses of Congress (S. 1128 and H. R. 2839) on May 20, 1872, by Senator Frederick A. Sawyer and Hon. Legrand W. Perce.

LXIV. The unanimous report of the Committee on Education and Labor of the House of Representatives on the bill above referred to; said committee consisting of Messrs. Legrand W. Perce, of Mississippi, chairman; George F. Hoar, of Massachusetts; Washington Townsend, of Pennsylvania; Roderick F. Butler, of Tennessee; Mark H. Dunnell, of Minnesota; Robert B. Elliott, of South Carolina; John B. Storm, of Pennsylvania; T. McIntyre, of Georgia; Hosea W. Parker, of New Hampshire; the report, submitted March 3, 1873, being in part as follows:

It is unnecessary to frame an argument to show the special importance of university culture in a country like ours, where the administration of public affairs, the molding of our political institutions, and hence the destinies of the Republic, are intrusted to representatives chosen by the people; where, moreover, as nowhere else, there must constantly arise new problems demanding the sure light of science, material, social, and political, for their solution. It is not enough that the American Republic be distinguished by the universality of common education; it should be no less distinguished by the prevalence of thorough culture. * * *

This need of the university has been felt and strongly expressed by many of the most distinguished citizens in all periods of our history. It was repeatedly declared by the framers of our national Constitution, and urged in the messages of the early Presidents; and although some of the colleges then in existence have largely increased their pecuniary foundations and enlarged their plans correspondingly, scientific discovery and the demands of the age have likewise so increased that the best of them still fall short of meeting the needs of the country and times. * * *

Nor has the recognition of this necessity for a true university been confined to individual writers. It was affirmed more than twenty years ago by an association of some of the most eminent men of the country, brought together solely by a mutual interest in this subject, and again, so recently as 1869, it was reaffirmed by the National Teachers' Association in convention assembled. * * *

Passing now from the question of need to the question of how that want is to be met, the committee are satisfied that it can not be by any institution at present existing, for these reasons:

(1) That none has or is likely to have the pecuniary resources essential to the highest and most complete university work.

(2) That none can be made so entirely free from objection on both denominational and local grounds as to insure the patronage of the people, regardless of section or partisan relationship.

(4) That no institution not established upon neutral ground, or other than national in the important sense of being established by the people and for the people of the whole nation, and in part for a national end, could possibly meet all the essential demands to be made upon it. * * *

The committee acknowledge the force of these views of the founders of the Government, and hence are prepared to indorse the sentiments expressed in the preamble to the bill under consideration, namely, that "it is the duty of every government to furnish to its people facilities for the highest culture," and that "such facilities can not be otherwise so well provided for the people of this nation as by founding a university so comprehensive in plan as to include every department of learning, so high as to embrace the limits of knowledge, so national in aim as to promote concord among all sections, and so related to other institutions as to promote their efficiency and with them form a complete system of American education."

It but remains, therefore, to determine whether the provisions of the bill are wisely adapted to the ends proposed.

The bill provides that the university shall be established at the national capital, where alone can be found convenient neutral ground in which the whole people of the United States have a common interest; where are annually gathered the representatives of every section of the country; where also are resident the representatives of all the foreign powers with whom we have intercourse; where are found to such an extent as nowhere else in this country most important auxiliaries in the form of the various government departments, literary, scientific, and industrial; and, finally, where alone the government has unquestioned authority to establish and maintain such an institution.

As to the government of the university, the plan is well calculated to command the confidence and support of the people of all portions of the country, to protect the institution from political interference, and to insure to its educational forces that freedom so essential to the life and growth of a university.

The bill provides for the organization of faculties embracing the present entire field of human knowledge, and opens the way for such modifications as will enable the institution to meet the demands of the future.

It wisely guards against the use of the people's money in aid of religious or political partisanship, and yet, under judicious safeguards, opens the door for instruction in every department of learning and in support of any principles of truth whatsoever.

It does not provide that the institution shall be absolutely free for students, * * * but in harmony with that freedom and elasticity which characterize the whole plan, it does provide that instruction shall at all times be as nearly free for students as consistent with the income of the institution and with the best interests of learning.

Another very important feature of this bill consists in the careful and impartial recognition it makes of all classes of our schools, which the university * * * will tend to stimulate, elevate, and harmonize, while at the same time supplying a crowning institution capable of supplementing their work and giving to the country a well-ordered system.

Hardly less important is the recognition the bill makes of the duty of the university to contribute to the advancement of knowledge * * * and the encouragement it provides by means of ordinary and honorary fellowships and other preferments to be awarded to such graduates as shall acquit themselves best during their respective courses of study, and to be conferred upon learned men of whatever institution or country who have shown distinguished ability for rendering the world valuable service in some of the various fields of research and investigation. Thus the plan of the university as to scope and adaptation to the true ends of such an institution as well as to the genius of the people for whom it is to be established, is comprehensive and complete.

The plan as to endowment is simple, definite, and secure; this, namely, that the Government shall bind itself to pay to the national university in perpetuity 5 per cent interest on a registered, unassignable certificate of $20,000,000, and that for so long a time as is necessary the accruing interest may be used for the purchase of grounds, the erection of needed buildings, and the equipment of the several departments of the institution.

The immense advantage to be derived from the relations to be established between the university and the numerous departments and bureaus of the Government will be apparent to any one familiar with the cost of furnishing and maintaining great libraries, scientific establishments, and collections illustrative of the arts and sciences, as will likewise the propriety of utilizing, for the purposes of education and national progress, facilities which could not otherwise be supplied without the expenditure of many millions. * * *

If, then, it be true, as the committee have briefly endeavored to show, that our country is at present wanting in the facilities for the highest culture in many departments of learning; and if it be true that a central university, besides meeting this demand, would quicken, strengthen, and systematize the schools of the country from the lowest to the highest; that it would increase the amount and the love of pure learning, now too little appreciated by our people, and so improve the intellectual and social status of the nation; that it would tend to homogeneity of sentiment, and thus strengthen the unity and patriotism of the people; that, by gathering at its seat distinguished savants, not only of our own but of other lands, it would eventually make of our national capital the intellectual center of the world, and so help the United States of America to rank first and highest among the enlightened nations of the earth; then is it most manifestly the duty of Congress to establish and amply endow such a university at the earliest possible day.

The committee, therefore, affirm their approval of the bill and recommend its passage by the House.[1]

LXV. Impromptu discussions of the national university proposition at the meeting of the National Educational Association, in 1873, at Elmira, N. Y.[2]

(1) Remarks of United States Senator G. W. Wright, of Iowa:

During the session of the last Congress a bill was introduced by Senator Howe which was broad in its scope and liberal in its endowment. No report was made upon Senator Howe's bill, but another bill, a few weeks later in the session, was introduced in the House and referred to the Committee on Education and Labor  This bill, after careful consideration, was unanimously reported to the House and its passage recommended. * * *

[1] H. of R., 42d Cong., 3d sess., Report No. 90.
[2] Proceedings Nat. Ed. Ass'n, 1873, pp. 120–129.

In the manner I have described the attention of Congress and of the people at large is turned to the accomplishment of this great object, which will prove to be the crowning glory of the first century of our national existence.

The city of Washington in a few years, under the skillful management of the board of public works, will become one of the most beautiful and attractive cities on this continent, and it is in the power of Congress, by the permanent establishment and liberal endowment of the national university, to make our national capital the intellectual center of the nations.

### (2) President James McCosh, of Princeton:

Although not approving of the bills referred to, I like the idea of a national university of a character so high that it would not be a competitor of any existing institution.

### (3) Superintendent Z. Richards, Washington, D. C.:

If the Government can do anything for education it surely can give the best kind of education. Our schools must be supported either by the State or by sects, or not at all. Schools we must have, but who wants purely sectarian schools only? * * * A candid and careful examination will hardly fail to convince any unbiased mind that these bills provide for that higher culture so much demanded, without interfering with our present colleges and so-called universities except to improve and elevate them, and without affecting the religious welfare of any denomination or sect.

### (4) President George P. Hays, Washington and Jefferson College, Pennsylvania:

I am much gratified at this discussion, for, whatever else it may do, it promotes the coming of an American university from some quarter. For that university, in some form and from some source, I am an earnest advocate. You will notice that while we have but one and the same thing in view, we are only at variance as to the method by which it is to be secured. One method is by the National Government and the other is by the transformation of some of our present colleges into the true university.

Is it doubted that there is a demand for such a university? That question has its answer indicated by the large numbers of our best graduates, looking to professorships and other scholarly positions, who go to Europe, by Professor Agassiz's school on the island in New England, and by the efforts of Harvard and Yale to establish a university course of lectures. * * *

But it is said, when there is a demand for such an institution it will come of itself. This reminds me of the man who replied, when asked for a contribution to a mission to the Jews, "The Jews give money to convert the Jews! Why the Jews are the richest people in the world. If they want to be converted, let them give the money themselves."

Moreover, as Dr. Reed, our president, says, "Logically it would seem as if education should begin and develop upward, while, as a fact, it begins at higher education and works downward." So, in all our history, we do not wait for State action until the whole people urge it, but act in view of the wants of the whole people. I am not so much afraid of the impurity of the Government. We are not near destruction; and there is virtue enough in the Republic to right its wrongs and carry on its work. I believe this university could be so managed, when established by Government, as to have a most beneficial effect on our educational system.

### (5) Remarks of W. B. Wedgewood, dean of the National University Law School, at Washington:

The act of Congress providing for the creation of corporations in the District of Columbia by the general law was approved May 5, 1870. The act provides the mode of establishing institutions of learning of the rank of a college or university. In accordance with these provisions, the National University, on the 19th day of September, 1870, became a body politic and corporate. * * *

This university, in the words of Madison, is "local in its legal character but universal in its beneficial effects." Following the advice of Washington, "that the primary object of such a national institution should be to educate our men in the science of government," its founders first established the law college for the education of those young men who, as statesmen and jurists, are to be the future guardians of the liberties of our country, as in the past they have been its heroic defenders.

The charter of the National University makes the President of the United States (*ex officio*) chancellor of the university. It first annual commencement was held at Lincoln Hall, on Tuesday evening, May 21, 1872. President Grant, in the presence of one of the most intelligent audiences ever assembled in Washington, conferred the degree of bachelor of laws upon a class of thirty-one young men, who had pursued their course of study for two years in the university.

## (6) President Daniel Read, University of Missouri:

That the national capital, in the territory under the immediate legislative control of Congress, was the only proper place for a national university, and that in this way only could the constitutional objection, which would be strong, * * * be obviated. But there were still other reasons for the location at the national capital—that there was the great Congressional Library, still to be increased from year to year; there was the astronomical observatory; there were vast collections in all departments from every part of the world; there were models in the arts, and besides scientific experiments were continually in progress for the purposes of the Government, to say nothing of the diplomatic and public discussions incident to the capital. All these means and advantages could be made available for a great institution of the kind proposed. * * *

Besides these considerations, the effect of such an institution would be beneficial upon the capital in elevating the general tone, in stimulating and concentrating scientific investigations, and awakening inquiry on social and economic questions. Many able young men connected with the Government as employés or attachés might be expected to avail themselves of the opportunity of attending the lectures, instructions, or experiments of such a university. It was a statement of a very able head of one of the Departments at Washington, that he could from any one of the Departments select a more learned faculty than any college in the land could boast of.

Surely no one would consider such an institution as any other than one for the highest scientific and literary culture of men who have already made attainments fitting them to enter upon a course of philosophic inquiry and scientific investigation. * * *

Then as to donations of land by the General Government for the encouragement and promotion of education; such gifts have been made almost from the beginning, even prior to the formation of the Federal Constitution. If I mistake not, the idea originated in good old Massachusetts, springing out of Massachusetts notions, * * * with Dr. Manasseh Cutler, the pastor of a church at Hamilton, not far from Cambridge, I believe. * * * This was as early as 1785. * * * Here is at least a historic argument in favor of aid from the General Government to institutions of education.

Now as to the idea itself of a national university, while as I have said, it is not specially my idea, * * * I can not treat as visionary that which Washington recommended, and James Madison and John Quincy Adams advocated, and many other great and patriotic men have zealously advocated as a means of elevating all our higher institutions of learning, and giving unity and concentration of effort to literary and scientific men, and constituting indeed a bond of unity to the nation itself. * * *

But this is not a question—I mean the education of the people as an interest of Government—to be argued in our day; we can not reverse American sentiment, which is growing stronger and stronger, and which now on this subject pervades the whole American people.

We must not fall into the error that the people are one thing and the Government something quite distinct and different, and having antagonistic interests. With us, government is nothing but an organized agency from the people, by the people, for the people.

LXVI. President Grant's recommendation, in his message of December 1, 1873, in these words:

I would suggest to Congress the propriety of promoting the establishment in this District of an institution of learning or university of the highest class, by donation of lands. There is no place better suited for such an institution than the national capital. There is no other place in which every citizen is so directly interested.[1]

LXVII. Further efforts of United States Senator Timothy O. Howe, of Wisconsin, especially—

(1) By sundry speeches wherein was urged the duty of the Government to make the fullest possible provision for the education of the people. As a matter of fact, every proposition to do anything in this interest had his sympathy and commanded his support, as may be inferred from the following passage from his speeches in the Senate:

I want to see a better style of men brought upon the stage of action just as soon as it is convenient. I do not expect, whether I leave these seats here early or late, ever to vote against the appropriation of a dollar which is asked for to aid in the work of human culture.

(2) By open and earnest advocacy of the proposed university in some of the public journals, for example, in the Wisconsin Journal of Education, in whose pages, upon more than one occasion, and especially in 1874, he presented its claims with all his accustomed clearness and logical force. From some of these papers are taken the extracts below:[2]

In the convention which framed the Constitution of the United States the subject of a national university was somewhat considered. The proposition had some warm friends. It found no enemies there. * * * It was in 1787 that James Madison, not of Massachusetts but of Virginia, not a professional teacher but a practical statesman, moved in convention, at Philadelphia, to clothe Congress with express powers to establish such a university.

To the Senator's mind the needs, duties, and powers of the nation were so very clear that the question of either, on the part of any intelligent citizen, awakened a suspicion of insincerity. If one showed himself critical as to details in any of the several bills, he would say:

Doubtless they are imperfect. It is the business of legislation and the work of time to perfect them. It is not to be expected that the first charter will be beyond the reach of criticism. The organic act of even Harvard was not. That ancient constitution was agreed to in the following words:

---

[1] House Ex. Docs., Forty-third Cong., 1st sess., Vol. I, pt. 1, p. 22.
[2] Wis. Jour. of Ed., Vol. IV, pp. 128–133, 161–164.

"The court agrees to give £400 towards a schoole or colledge, whereof £200 to be paid next yeare and £200 when the work is finished, and the nex court to appoint wheare and what building."

On that slight foundation was started what has since become the present noble institution. Had the statesmen of Massachusetts then urged the defects in that charter, we might never have been permitted to rejoice in the existence of Harvard. * * *

The great question is, Shall the nation establish a university? Doubtless there are those who may think the expenditure demanded by such an enterprise is beyond the present ability of the legislature. * * * There may be those who think the founding of such an institution is outside of the constitutional authority of the National Government. * * * There may be those who think the provision already made for intellectual culture is sufficient. * * *

For all such the Senator was ready with those noble words of Horace Mann:

In our country and our time no man is worthy the honored name of statesman who does not include the *highest practicable education* of the people in all his plans of administration. He may have eloquence, he may have a knowledge of all history, jurisprudence, and by them he might claim in other countries the elevated rank of a statesman; but unless he speaks, plans, labors at all times and in all places for the culture and education of the whole people, he is not, he can not be, an American statesman.

If some caviler should claim that he did not mean to exclude all governments from the work of education, but only to exclude the Government of the United States, he would say:

His argument is not consistent, nor could an argument consistent with that view be framed. Manifestly education is a matter of private concern only or it is a matter of public concern also. If of private concern, it should be left to the individual, and all governments should let it alone. But if of public concern, government should attend to it; not any one government exclusively, but every government clothed with any authority over the public welfare should contribute to the work according to its ability and its opportunity. Undoubtedly, under our political system, the work is left mainly to the several States, but if the National Government can help, it should.

Did it appear that there was no disposition to exclude government from the work of primary, and only from that of higher education, he would reply:

Still, the fact remains that the education of the citizen is of value to the State or it is not. If it be conceded that partial education is of some value, it will hardly be denied that thorough education is of more value. Besides it is in this precise way that the builders of the National Government intended it should aid the cause of mental culture. *It was in this precise way that Washington and Madison (and Jefferson) so incessantly urged the Government to act.* * * *

The government of Massachusetts has faithfully seconded the aspirations of her people. The governments of other States have faithfully reflected the indifference of theirs. The government of Massachusetts can not directly aid the people of Delaware, nor can the government of Delaware directly retard the people of Massachusetts. Yet these two communities are by no means independent; the people of each State influence the destiny of the people in every other State.

A vote given in Rhode Island may destroy the profits of a harvest in the valley of the Mississippi. A vote given in Kansas may throw Wall street into convulsions.

A million and a half of such votes are in the hands of men utterly unable to read them. Under such circumstances can the nation afford to fold its arms? It may be well enough when you are safe on shore, if you see a ship in the offing with a stone-blind crew on her deck and a tempest about to break over her men, to call on the helpless seamen to make sail and come into port. The world will not be apt to call such obdurate selfishness blessed, but they may call it discreet, prudent, economical. If, on the contrary, you are not on shore, but in the cabin of the imperiled ship, you must not expect to earn a high character for prudence even unless you help the sightless mariners to handle the ropes, or at least show them the way to the shrouds. * * * * When Shreveport and Memphis are wasted by fever, when Ireland is wasted by famine, and Chicago and Boston by fire, Government has afforded relief, although not expressly assigned to that duty, and although relief was otherwise attainable. Government has built many school-houses. * * * It has endowed noble universities and agricultural colleges, * * * although private agencies might possibly have done the same.

Public liberty still survives. It is less than a quarter of a century since Daniel Webster looked with apprehension upon the prospect of a separate republic on the Pacific Coast. The Government has helped to bind the two coasts together by a railway. Perhaps it is too early to say what will be the effect of that measure upon American liberty. But it is more than two hundred years since Government laid the corner stone of Harvard University, and it is not yet perceptible that the foundations of public liberty have been weakened thereby.

Among the aborigines of America, statesmen do very generally hold that public authority should defer to private agencies; and so their Government looks cooly on while the victim of larceny makes reprisal on the thief, and the friends of the murdered execute vengeance on the murderer. But the prevailing opinion in American society is, that all such excentricities as larceny and homicide call for the admonition and instruction of the Government. Not that private agencies can not reach them; Government will not allow such agencies to interfere. The great teachers, the Government commissions for the instruction of such learners are courts, penitentiaries, and the gallows. Very many people believe the schoolhouse and the university to be means of instruction quite as becoming and much cheaper; and there are some enthusiasts (?) who believe that such means, properly employed, are quite as efficient and do not sap the foundations of public liberty any more than their more popular rivals—prisons and gibbets.

We deceive ourselves dangerously, says one, when we think or speak as if education, whether primary or university, could guarantee republican institutions. Do we, indeed? Well, educate a people once—not a class, but a people—and then let some cocked hat or some crowned head attempt to establish any other than republican institutions over them, and see who is dangerously deceived!

## LXVIII. The address of Dr. Andrew D. White, president of Cornell University, at the Detroit meeting of the National Association in 1874.

On their foundation I would have public grants and private gifts combined. Here too, fortunately, there is a well-defined national policy and to some extent a State policy.

The National Government acted in accordance with it when it gave the grant of lands for general and scientific and industrial education in 1862, and the States acted in accordance with it when they appropriated that grant—Connecticut to Yale, New Hampshire to Dartmouth, Vermont to the Vermont University, New Jersey to Rutgers, Massachusetts to the State Agricultural College and Institute of Technology, Rhode Island to Brown University. The Scripture rule in this case is "to him that hath shall be given." The scientific rule is, let there be a "survival of the fittest," and the plain rule of common sense—whether in Nation or State, whether in old

States or new—whether for public or private gifts, is for primary education, diffusion; for advanced education, concentration of resources.

And as to the general application of these rules, the history of all civilized nations and especially our own, shows that the thoughtful statesmanship of each generation should provide for the primary, secondary and advanced education of each.

Accepting this principle the immediate care should evidently be to strengthen by public action the best foundations for advanced education which we already have; and should the National Government take a few of the strongest in various parts of the country, and by greater endowments still, make them national universities, or should it create one or more new ones worthy of the nation, placing one of them at the national capital, where the vast libraries, museums, and laboratories of various sorts now existing may be made of use for advanced instruction, and where the university could act directly and powerfully for good in sending graduates admirably prepared into the very heart and center of our national civil service, to elevate and strengthen it, I believe in spite of pessimists and doctrinaires that the result would tell vastly for good upon the whole country.[1]

LXIX. The efforts of John Hancock, superintendent of the Cincinnati public schools, in an address before the National Educational Association at its annual meeting of 1874, at Detroit, in which he said:

The design of the National University should not be to do the work now done by the sectarian and small colleges, but to do the work of a kind that they, with their want of facilities for it, can not do. In other words, we need a national university to complete the higher education begun in these colleges, no matter whether they are sectarian or not; and if sectarian, no matter what their sect may be. It has been claimed that the freedom of the American citizen would in some way be infringed, and that he would lose the spirit of independent self-help if the Government should extend him aid in his efforts to obtain the best education by establishing a school of learning under its own control. I must confess such fears oppress me but little. The freedom bought by ignorance is of but little worth. Besides, the argument would apply to every grade of public schools and prove more than those who use it intend.

But, as I have already said, whatever may be our theory as to State aid in education, the practice of the nation has been sufficiently declared. It has recently aided agricultural, mechanical, and liberal education by a generous grant of public lands for the purpose; and many of the States, and conspicuously the one we are in to-day, are reaping an abundant harvest from this generosity. Will any one dare say that it would have been a better disposition of these lands to give them to great railroad corporations, with Credit Mobilier and general political demoralization as a result?

Give us, then, the National University to attract young men to enter upon careers of higher culture and living, and into it will gather from all the small colleges of the country youth already trained to correct habits of investigation, who will enter upon original work in every department of human knowledge—of which work we have hitherto had so little—backed by the wealth of the nation. And with such facilities as she can afford, we need entertain no fears that her sons will fail to give a good account of themselves.[2]

LXX. The efforts of Dr. W. T. Harris (now national Commissioner of Education) in sundry ways, but especially in the address by him at Detroit, on occasion of the annual meeting of the National Educational Association, in 1874, from which the following passages are taken:

Turning now to the demand that arises for a national university we encounter two

---

[1] Proceedings Nat. Ed. Ass'n, 1874, p. 73.          [2] Id., p. 77.

new problems: (1) What shall be its relation to the existing collegiate institutions, some 300 in number? (2) What shall be its relation to our National Government?

Our oldest and best colleges are all aspiring to the organization which will entitle them to the name of university. They have very many professors of such high and rare qualifications as would make them worthy of places on the faculty of a national university. But a chief source of complaint with them now is that the degrees which they award mean nothing by reason of the fact that in the poorest colleges one may get a degree for qualifications which would not entitle him even to enter the most advanced college.

In a system of city schools the one high school measures and reduces to the same standard all the district schools. Just in this manner would a great national university measure and reduce to a common standard all the collegiate institutions in the land. Thus the best institutions of this sort now existing would receive the most benefit from such a university, in the fact that their high standard would have unquestionable attestation. Inferior colleges would be obliged to limit their attempts to what they could do with a reasonable standard of perfection. Their pretensions would collapse to the solid reality. In a few years the whole country would have arrived at a sort of specie basis, so far as college diplomas are concerned.

But the most obvious and often repeated objection to the proposed national university is drawn from the nature of our national politics. It is contended that we have a certain low standard of politics, and that whatever is directed, managed, and supported by the state, suffers inevitably from political influence. A university founded under the management of our National Government would be the prey of demagogues, it is thought. This view is developed and supported chiefly by those who hold the theory that our Government should exclude from its functions an interference with education or with other functions within the range of civil society. This theory has been persistently reiterated in political platforms and political treatises during the period since the formation of our Federal Government. At times it has led to legislation tending to purge away certain complications with civil society, which have arisen through various exigencies of war or peace. The history of legislation regarding a national bank, regarding the issue of paper money, or a tariff, regarding various internal improvements and the status of corporations, is one of the most momentous interest to the thinking statesman and economist. Whatever violent legislation has attempted, to purge the state of all complication with civil society, has failed. Again and again in our history we have come upon conditions which necessitated the interference of Government in affairs of civil society. In latter years, and in proportion as the relations of civil society have become more complex with us, such complication has become more and more frequent and inevitable. Internal improvements, foreign and domestic commerce, intercommunication, money, bonds, and corporate rights and privileges—the General Government can not choose but mediate in those things. Its war caused it to create a mercantile commodity in the shape of bonds to the amount of thousands of millions of dollars, and throw the same on the market of the world within a period of six years. Civil society and the state are only different phases of the same organic human combination; in the former, in civil society, the individual uses the organization for his own sustenance and support, and the furtherance of his private ends through the agency of wealth; in the latter, the state, the organization, exists in its unity, and subordinates all individuals to its end.

The State must exist as the logical condition of the existence of civil society and the welfare or rational existence of the individual. Unless the individual devotes his life and property to the state and acknowledges the supreme right to use him and his he does not properly recognize his position. But it exists whether consciously recognized or not by the citizen or statesman. Now, from the reciprocal relation of the functions of the state and civil society as related to the individual, it follows that the state as a directive power of the organism as a whole must legislate regarding all such phases as relate to its own self-preservation and perpetuation. No other people ever before started such a theory as the one which asserts or presupposes in some form the denial of an organic relation of state and society. So long as we undertake to realize this theory we shall act a farce before ourselves and the intelligence of mankind. We shall do practically in spite of ourselves what we condemn in theory.

By a common movement the foremost nations of Europe have advanced to the position that public education is a concern that vitally interests the state. No state can allow its productive industry to fall behind that of other nations. Independence can not be long preserved on such terms. Directly, as necessary to the war material, and indirectly as essential to productive industry, the education of the whole people is indispensable, and the Government can not afford to leave it to arbitrary private benevolence or to the zeal of the church.

The great desideratum in this country is to kindle still more the zeal of our legislators on behalf of public education. To attempt to cool their zeal is to work a mischief. It behooves our Government to see to it that education is national and not sectional or sectarian, or a matter of caste. On no other nation is this injunction laid so heavily. The foundations of our Government rest on popular education. Other nations have always seen to it that their directive intelligence was educated at the expense of the state. They even go farther in our time and educate their sinews of war and the quality of their productive industry. We, in America, are committed to universal public education implicitly by the constitution of our Government, which is a Government of the people by the people. Not only must the citizen here be able to read and interpret the laws of the land for himself, but he is expected to possess and exercise the requisite intelligence to make the laws which he is to obey. All the evils which we suffer politically may be traced to the existence in our midst of an immense mass of ignorant, illiterate, or semi-educated people who assist in governing the country, while they possess no insight into the true nature of the issues which they attempt to decide. If in Europe, and even in China, the directive classes are educated at public expense, how essential is it that the Republican state shall before all insure universal education within its domain!

*　　　*　　　*　　　*　　　*　　　*　　　*

The incompatibility of the ideas on which the two systems of schools—the public schools and the college preparatory schools—are based, may be apparent from the brief statements here presented. A thorough consideration of the subject would exhibit more fully how it is that our colleges, as at present constituted, do not fully answer the needs of this country at this time. The problems of sociology and statesmanship, the philosophy of science, of literature, of history, of jurisprudence, these demand the concentrated labor of a large corps of salaried professors provided for at well-endowed colleges and universities.

It is in this respect that the National University, founded by the American state and endowed munificently, would prove of the greatest value to the community. It would emancipate our public schools from the two-fold danger: (a) the danger from the influence of the colleges against the continuation of a liberal education when begun in the public high school; (b) the danger of a course of study in the common schools that dissipates the energies of the pupil by neglecting the disciplinary studies and substituting therefor a mere smattering of natural science. The National University, with its endowed professorships and fellowships, would furnish the desired center for free untrammeled study into the philosophy of those branches which are taught only in their elements even in the best colleges. It is the general views that we need in our higher education. A training in the philosophy of literature, history, and sciences can be obtained now only in German universities; but this would be the special function of our National University. Methodology is the final topic in the course of study; to understand the general relations of a branch, and its method of evolution, is the best thing to be learned; to give such insight is the province of the university. Whatever want of adaptation between our common schools and higher schools might arise, would speedily become manifest through the highest link of our system and its causes would be remedied.

As to the influence of a national university upon our National Government, this would obviously be salutary. Properly protected from sudden legislation, it would soon grow to be an object of national pride, and it would exert a molding influence upon education in all the States just in proportion to its achievements and rank. The Representatives of each State in Congress would learn through it the types and models of educational institutions which they would become zealous to found at home among their constituents. Secondary education, at present sustained by so precarious a tenure by the several State and municipal governments, would become firm and secure through the influence of a national university in educating the ideas and feelings of politicians into the support of a complete system of public education as a necessary concomitant of democratic self-government. It is impossible to conceive of a more efficient influence in favor of education in this country. It would effect far more than the proposed grant of the proceeds of all our public-school lands to the school funds of the several States. The great want of our time is not a funded endowment of education in the several States, but a conviction in the minds of the people and their representatives of the essential importance of a complete system of free education supported by public taxation. This conviction alone will render us safe.

It is the trite lament of our time that our Government needs purifying; that it should be surrounded by elevating influences. It is the mistake of certain abstract political theorists in this country, who would attempt to purify the Government by divorcing it from the concrete relation to civil society, that has prevented the growth of a science of statesmanship here and has caused the humiliating spectacle of acts of corruption done through sheer ignorance of the proprieties of statesmanship.

When we consider the great advantages that would ensue from the connection that a national university would have with the several bureaus of our General Government, and of the digested results that would proceed from the investigation of the statistical data there collected from the various phases of our social political life; when we consider the effect of collecting, by means of a vast endowment, the best educated intelligence of the time in a university faculty, and the resulting study of our institutions by free disinterested investigation, elevated above the atmosphere of strife wherein the practical every-day world is immersed, the importance of this movement to found a national university is fully apparent. Its advent will correct and prevent wrong tendencies in the direction of common schools, and likewise of colleges and private schools. It will be the source of supply for teachers and professors who shall take up the work of secondary education in the several States. From its lecture rooms will emanate the science that will solve our social and political problems, and furnish the philosophy for a true statesmanship.[1]

LXXI. The speech of Rev. Dr. George P. Hays, president of Washington and Jefferson College, at the meeting of the National Educational Association at Detroit in 1874:

For my part I am earnestly, heartily for a national university by any means that will give us success. We do not want another institution chartered as a university but doing only collegiate work. We do not want a national university with any such pitiful income as two or three hundred thousand dollars. As I understand it, what the friends of this project seek is an institution devoted exclusively to true university or post-graduate work, to whose privileges all may come on equal terms, but where none shall be candidates for its degrees without the diploma of some college of recognized standing, or after such an examination as shall enable the university

---

[1] Proceedings Nat. Ed. Ass'n., 1874, pp. 82, 86.

itself to confer the bachelor's degree. This institution ought to have an income of at least $1,000,000, and so be able to subdivide the fields of study and call to its chairs fit men to work them up until the best instruction to be found among men may be had here.

Have we no national pride, that, having outstripped the peoples of the old world, we must yet be tied to them as our schoolmasters? Every year we have hundreds in Europe at their universities. * * * I blush for my country when I see her expending her millions for a centennial which shall leave no permanent fountain of progress behind, and remember what untold thousands she has squandered on improvements built by fraud, and see that American folly of a bald unfinished pile of marble—the mockery of a monument to Washington—and think that a national university is opposed on grounds of economy! It is time we should rise to the recognition of our duty to progress and civilization; and I congratulate the president of Cornell, that, though he is at the head of a rich institution, he is above the littleness of a jealousy that seems to be suggested elsewhere through fear lest something be put within the reach of our people better than themselves.

We patronize science in a cheap way in this country. We have sacrificed Kane and Hall in a hunt for the north pole, and we have now a few men at national expense looking at the transit of Venus, but our aping of scientific manners, while we found no unsurpassed university, is like the poor man who sent his son to a rich man's house "with a patch on both knees and gloves on." I may not be able to help this cause greatly, but my country shall have what I can give to obtain a university with the men and means to open to the world a place of learning taking the first rank in scholarship and pervaded with the best spirit of American life, social, political, and religious[1].

LXXII. The address of John W. Hoyt, before the higher department of the National Educational Association, at its annual meeting held at Detroit in 1874. From said address, the concluding passages:

Certainly no American will deny that self-reliance is an essential element of individual manhood, as well as of a noble national character. It is precisely for this reason, among others, that we urge the duty of the Government to care for the highest practical education of the whole people. For there is no dependence so abject as that of a profoundly ignorant man or nation; no self-reliance so complete and royal as that which comes of intelligence. Ignorance is slavery; knowledge is power and independence. * * * * * * *

As I understand it, the Government of this country is nothing very different from a trusteeship or agency, established by the whole people for the public convenience and for permanent as well as present advantage. The Constitution is a binding agreement of the people as to the purpose and organization of this agency, the kind of agents to be employed, the manner of their choosing, and the nature and scope of the duties they are to perform.

Cherishing the theory of self-reliance, the people have not usually deemed it duty or wisdom to take of their common substance and give to the individual citizen or the individual State, even when such giving would promote a necessary public object, unless it has seemed very clear that such object could not, or pretty certainly would not be attained without the national aid. But who will say that the people, acting through this agency—the Government—are not both competent and in duty bound to lend the public aid to all such enterprises not in conflict with expressed provisions of the Constitution, and in acknowledged harmony with its whole spirit and purpose, as are by them, the people, deemed essential to the general welfare, and as are either not possible of accomplishment without that aid, or, being possible, are in great danger of being too long delayed?

---

[1] Proceedings of Nat. Ed. Ass'n, 1874, p. 98.

Admitting, for the sake of the argument, the full force of the doctrine of some, that government is not to do a public good even unless that good be otherwise unattainable, the argument is still good for nothing against the object we seek to accomplish, since it is a public good otherwise unattainable. Primary schools there would be without public aid, but they would be scattering in location, irregular and inefficient in their work, and worst of all, utterly wanting in many cases where most needed. Colleges there would be, as any one may see who looks abroad, but except here and there, when particularly favored with the accumulations of generations or the princely gift of a noble man, they must of necessity have a sickly life and do a feeble work. While of a great university, with its vast array of auxiliary establishments, its multitude of learned professors, and its requisite annual income of a million and more, it is hardly necessary to say the hope of such an institution on any merely private, denominational, or even State foundation must be long deferred.

Last of all, if the question of means were not involved there is one broad reason why this public good, the schools the country needs, including the university, are otherwise unattainable, this, namely, that if established and maintained in sufficient number, and of every class and rank, by private means, they would still not be public schools, wholly free from the warping influence of private or denominational aims of whatever sort, institutions equally open to all qualified candidates, as well as purely consecrated to the culture of the people, and to the advancement of science and learning among men.   *   *   *

The Government cannot now repudiate or reverse its beneficent educational policy. The logic of facts and of reason will not permit it to stop short of the most complete provision for every department of American education. The people are growing in their realization of the necessity there is for insuring the best possible education of the masses. The variety and vastness of the national resources and the rapid progress of other nations are making a strong and growing demand upon the industrial arts, which they are powerless to meet without the help of the best technical schools; while the conspicuous place we hold among the great nations of the earth, the nature of our Government, and the genius and aspirations of our people are reasons deep and urgent for a high and thorough culture that must early move the nation to adopt measures that will give to the United States a true university.[1]   *   *   *

LXXIII. The action of the National Educational Association at the concluding general session of its said annual meeting of 1874, in unanimously adopting the following resolution:

*Resolved,* That this Association does hereby reaffirm its former declarations in favor of the establishment of a national university devoted not to collegiate but to university work, providing higher instruction in all departments of learning, and so organized as to secure the necessary independence and permanency in its management.[2]

Forgetting for the moment that the committee appointed at the St. Louis meeting in 1872 was to be "a permanent committee," the association also adopted the following resolution:

*Resolved,* That a committee of this association consisting of thirteen members, be appointed to lay this subject before Congress, with power to appoint a subcommittee in each State for coöperative effort.[2]

The committee so appointed was to consist of the following persons:

John W. Hoyt, Madison, Wis.; Andrew D. White, New York; John Hancock, Ohio; Wm. T. Harris, Missouri; David A. Wallace, Illinois; Mark Hopkins, Massa-

---

[1] Proceedings Nat. Ed. Ass'n, 1874, pp. 183–7.        [2] Id. pp. 138, 139.

chusetts; Joseph Henry, Washington City; J. P. Wickersham, Pennsylvania; W. F. Phelps, Minnesota; D. F. Boyd, Louisiana; Alex. Hogg, Alabama; E. E. White, Ohio; Geo. P. Hays, Pennsylvania; Z. Richards, District of Columbia.[2]

LXXIV. The American Journal of Education, published at St. Louis, has ever been an advocate of the university proposition. In illustration, the following passages from the January number, 1875:

It must always be a subject of regret that the convention which framed our constitution voted down the proposition [to include a provision] for the establishment of a national university. We hail the revival of such a measure now with joy.

\*      \*      \*

We need the minds, and, therefore, must rear the minds which can push forward this frontier of knowledge, so as to bring these truths with all their benefactions from the further to the hither side, from the barren possibility of being enjoyed into actual realized enjoyment.

And this is just what a national university will accomplish for the people of these United States. By its location at the national capital, by its vast endowment and array of distinguished ability, by its nationality and by the high attainments demanded for admission to its privileges, it will furnish us the minds that would otherwise be delayed in their appearance, to open to us the treasures that lie buried in nature's beneficent storehouse awaiting the genius of some scientific Columbus to lead the way to their utilization or multiplied adaptations to the diversified wants of man.

LXXV. A tour of the country by John W. Hoyt, in 1875, and personal interviews by him with leading friends of education in nearly all the States east of the Rocky Mountains, to the end of a systematic and unremitting effort in support of the university proposition; also, efforts at Washington, in 1876, in connection with the revival of the bill favorably reported by the Congressional committee of the House of Representatives in March, 1873—efforts finally thwarted by the excitement growing out of the electoral contest and by other circumstances occasioning a further postponement.

LXXVI. The recommendation of President R. B. Hayes, in his message of December 3, 1877, to wit:

The wisdom of legislation upon the part of Congress in the aid of the States for the education of the whole people in those branches of study which are taught in the common schools of the country is no longer a question. The intelligent judgment of the country goes still further, regarding it as also both constitutional and expedient for the General Government to extend to technical and higher education such aid as is deemed essential to the general welfare and to our due prominence among the enlightened and cultivated nations of the world.

It is encouraging to observe in connection with the growth of fraternal feeling in those States in which slavery formerly existed evidences of increasing interest in universal education; and I shall be glad to give my approval to any appropriate measure which may be enacted by Congress for the purpose of supplementing with national aid the local systems of education in those States and in all the States; and having already invited your attention to the needs of the District of Columbia with respect to its public-school system, I here add that I believe it desirable, not so much with reference to the local wants of the District, but to the great and lasting benefit of the entire country, that this system should be crowned with a university in

[1] Proceedings Nat. Ed. Assn., 1874, p. 138.      [2] Id., p. 139.

all respects in keeping with the national capital and thereby realize the cherished hopes of Washington on this subject.[1]

LXXVII. President Hayes' message of December 2, 1878, in which occurs this passage:

To education more than to any other agency we are to look as the resource for the advancement of the people in the requisite knowledge and appreciation of their rights and responsibilities as citizens; and I desire to repeat the suggestion contained in my former message in behalf of the enactment of an appropriate measure by Congress for the purpose of supplementing with national aid the local systems of education in the several States.[2]

LXXVIII. The Journal of Education, published at Boston, in its issue of February 3, 1881, supports the university proposition in these terms:

But whoever carefully considers the present growth of Washington as an educational center, can not resist the conviction that, in the fullness of time this vision of the fathers will also "materialize," and the national university, perhaps in some original plan of organization, will become an accomplished fact. Meanwhile it is interesting to see how rapidly the conditions are being proposed, and the materials accumulated for a university of broader scope than has yet been established. * * * It is not difficult to see, if these things go on for ten years to come as in the past, that in a perfectly natural way a central faculty of examination will get itself established as a national university, conferring degrees, arranging courses of study, giving not only to the residents of Washington, but attracting the aspiring youth of every portion of the country. Then will be realized, even in a grander way than the fathers imagined, some of the noblest dreams of that wonderful group of men who founded the Republic. The more we study the career of the dozen leading minds of that first revolutionary epoch, the more are we compelled to admire their prophetic foresight. We are just coming to the point in national affairs where we glimpse the vast horizon which bounded their wide survey. Unless we mistake, the coming few years are to realize, in the education of the people, some of their loftiest dreams.

LXXIX. Advocacy of the national university proposition by Hon. L. Q. C. Lamar in his report as Secretary of the Interior, for the fiscal year ending January 30, 1885, wherein he said:

Eighty years ago President Jefferson, then in the fullest tide of his authority as a party chief, told Congress that to complete the circle of Democratic policy a national university was a necessity and should at once be created. In this he followed the recommendations of his predecessors, Washington and Adams, the former of whom ten years before declared that the desirableness of a national university had so constantly increased with every new view he had taken of the subject that he could not omit the opportunity of recalling the attention of Congress to its importance. Mr. Madison, in 1810, renewed the recommendation, with the declaration that such an institution would contribute not less to strengthen the foundations than to adorn the structure of our free and happy system of government, and that it would be universal in its beneficial effects.

This national institution which Washington, Adams, Jefferson, and Madison thought so necessary has never been established; and in these later years the idea of a national university constitutes no part of the plans of statesmen and seems to have been lost sight of by the people.

In the meantime scientific bureaus have grown up one by one under the Government, with observatories, laboratories, museums, and libraries, until the whole range

[1] Cong. Record, 45th Cong., 2d sess., Vol. 7, p't. I., p. 7.
[2] Cong. Record, 45th Cong., 3d sess., Vol. 8, p't. I., p. 7.

of physical science is represented by national institutions established by the Government for the purpose of prosecuting researches embracing astronomy, meteorology, geography of land and sea, geology, chemistry, statistics, mechanical inventions, etc. If the various commissions, bureaus, and divisions of the Executive Departments at Washington which have for their object the prosecution of scientific research could be combined as integral parts of one scientific institution, such an institution would be of greater proportions and more comprehensive than any other in the world; and should a university be erected thereon, with a superstructure commensurate with the foundation, it would be without a rival in any country.

The common-school system, designed to furnish every citizen with an education which ought to be a strict necessity for his daily work of life, constitutes the foundation of our democracy. But this is not enough to satisfy its instincts. In the history of nations democracies have been the cradles of pure thought and art. The same cause which operated in them exists in American society, and whether through a national university or in fragmentary institutions in the several States, sooner or later a higher education, higher than the common school or the academy or the college can furnish, will alone realize and express the higher aspirations of American democracy.[1]

LXXX. The advocacy of the university idea by Rev. Dr. A. D. Mayo, in Education, March number, 1885:

A new claim to our admiration of the father of our country is found in a review of his life and opinions on the theme which is now so rapidly coming to the front in our national life—the education of the people.

*       *       *       *       *       *       *

But his favorite educational idea was a national university, to be located in the national capital, under the auspices and supervision of the General Government. * * *

According to the best ideals and the imperative necessities of a century ago, this plan of Washington was one of the greatest thoughts of the new American life. * * *

But this noble design of Washington has never been realized, partly from the sharp rivalries of States, localities, and religious bodies, jealous of a great central institution that would overshadow them all. Those rivalries only multiplied by the vast and unexpected growth of the country. But there are other and larger reasons for the failure. Within the past century the idea of university life and of the higher education has greatly changed. The contacts of college life have greatly enlarged. A whole hemisphere of elaborate culture—to some the most important hemisphere—has been added to the narrow curriculum of classics, mathematics, and philosophy of that day; the varied departments of physical studies, and the industrial, technical, and artisan training developed by applied science and inventive skill; with immense expansion in the realm of history, philology, literature, music, and the fine arts; and, not inferior in importance to any, the science and art of instruction. It is doubtful if any university, however magnificently endowed, even supported by national patronage, could possibly assume the direction of the whole circle of the higher education as understood to-day. This can only be understood by groups of schools, generously endowed, supervised by experts, and, at best, connected with each other by a bond that is little more than an abstract name. * * *

Every large American city has its special merit, and many of them are superior in certain lines of power, culture, and virtue to the city of Washington. But Washington is the only city which is growing to be metropolitan under the sole influence

---

[1] Report Sec. of Int. for 1885, p. 86.

of the national idea. This is the one spot in the Union where no man can safely put on airs of local superiority; where State and sectional pride are of little account; where religious sects and social cliques, and even the sharp distinctions of country and race, all subside in the presence of the majestic nationality which, like a gracious mother, assures to its children the largest freedom, with only the strong compulsion of the law that shall make our people one. So here, if anywhere, must we look for the realization of what Washington saw in vision.

LXXXI. Advocacy of the proposition, in the International Review for December, 1885, by Lester F. Ward. In commenting upon references to the recommendation of Hon. L. Q. C. Lamar, Secretary of the Interior, in his report of 1885, Mr. Ward says:

But a true university is not a mere school for the training of great numbers of young people. It is an institution in which the most perfect appliances for original research may be brought together, and where a few who are able and willing to avail themselves of them may have the opportunity to do so. The tenor of the Secretary's report clearly shows that this is what he contemplated by a national university. He regards the existing scientific bureaus of the Government, with all their apparatus and appliances, as the "foundation" upon which to erect a university as a "superstructure," thus making a positive aid to the necesssary research that the Government must carry on. The whole would thus become a great American institute, analogous in some respects to the Institute of France.[1]

LXXXII. The article on a national university by G. G. H., dated January 1, 1886, and published in Vol. VII, p. 12, of Science.

LXXXIII. The contributions of Dr. Charles Kendall Adams, president of Cornell University, in an address on "Washington and the Higher Education," delivered on February 22, 1888; from which the following quotations are made:

The time when the Federal Government was formed was the occasion when provision should have been made for education in all of its grades. But the golden opportunity was lost. A few saw the

" Tide in the affairs of men
Which, taken at the flow, leads on to fortune,"

but the number was too few to accomplish any result. Alas! that the next generations were to realize that

"The golden opportunity
Is never offered twice."

If there were not wanting a few who saw the need of more general and systematic provisions for higher education, I think it may justly be said that there were only two whose efforts are worthy of note—Jefferson and Washington—the one through his successful endeavors to establish a university of character in his own State, the other through a still loftier though unsuccessful desire to found a national university at the national capital. * * *

The next contribution of Jefferson to the cause of higher education in America was still more characteristic of his fertile and peculiar genius. It was that interesting proposal of his to take up one of the European universities and transplant it to the soil of the United States. * * *

But the Genevan episode, though in itself it never for a moment had any prospect of success, was not without one important result. It performed the service of calling

---

attention to the weakness of the prevailing educational system. It tended to clear the atmosphere of the haziness on educational questions that everywhere seemed to prevail. Most important of all, it brought Washington to a decision on one important question concerning which, for a considerable time, he had been in doubt. If he did not turn the scheme lightly aside, as a project of no importance, we must suppose it was because of the really serious and elaborate importunities of Jefferson.

The father of the project knew that Washington had contemplated an important gift toward the establishment of a national university. But even Jefferson's importunities failed to shake the wise judgment of Washington. The idea of a national university he was indeed in favor of. But the objections to the Swiss project seemed to him insurmountable. He distinctly avowed his unwillingness to subordinate the idea of an American university to a foreign body of professors, even were they, as a body, to constitute the most learned faculty in Europe. He declared that a foreign importation en masse might preclude some of the first professors in other countries from participation in the proposed national university. In short, while insisting that the new university should be distinctively American in character, he took a broadly international view of the subject, and declared that they ought to hold themselves free to choose the ablest professors, in whatever country they were to be found.   *   *   *

Washington announced his views and purposes on many different occasions. There are two or three utterances, however, which contain so much wisdom, as well as clearness of purpose, that no mere abstract can do them justice, and, therefore, I beg to quote the passages in full.

Before doing so, however, I would call your attention to the three reasons embodied in the extracts I shall quote. The first is a postulate, not so much expressed as taken for granted, that special, and careful, and somewhat elaborate training in governmental affairs is necessary to the political welfare of the country. In the second place, he deplores in express terms the going abroad of so many young men to complete their education, since, in their formative days, they are likely to imbibe political principles antagonistic to the institutions under which they are to live. And, in the third place, as if anticipating the very misunderstandings and prejudices that formed so large an element in bringing about our civil war, he dwells especially upon the importance of bringing the youth from all parts of the country to a common educational center of higher learning, in order that, "by freedom of intercourse," and "collision of sentiment," their misunderstandings and prejudices may be worn away.   *   *   *

Thus fully did Washington set forth his views. With what wisdom and prescience did he behold what was before the country! He foresaw the sectional jealousies that were likely to arise, and he sought to avert them. He deplored the alienation from republican institutions that would spring up in immature minds, educated under foreign skies. He saw, and again and again proclaimed, the necessity of thorough and elaborate instruction in the science of government, and he ardently desired that the necessity of going to foreign lands for such instruction should be obviated. He knew that private benevolence, even if supplemented with the resources of the States, would be inadequate to establish the needed institution. He saw that, of all forms of government, those which are most dependent upon the intelligence and morality of the people, must make the most careful provision for education in morality and intelligence. He was fully aware that the ends which he sought could not be attained without the help of secondary as well as university education, and, therefore, he divided his gift between a preparatory school in Virginia, and a university at the national capital.

Thus we see that he labored under no such pestilent delusion as to suppose that an education in the mere rudiments of knowledge is a guaranty against the political dangers that were to be averted. It was a university—a university in the broadest and highest sense of the term, that was the peculiar object of his educational solicitude.

There is something in the persistency and the nobility of Washington's thought on the subject of a national university that reminds us of what occurred only ten years later at the capital of one of the nations of Europe. Prussia had fallen under the contemptuous displeasure of Napoleon; had been humiliated and well nigh destroyed. Despoiled of her fortresses robbed of half her territory, her army, even for purposes of defense, reduced to a handful of men, to her more than to any other of Napoleon's foes, it had been permitted

" To read the book of fate,
And see the revolution of the times
Make mountains level, and the continent,
Weary of solid firmness, melt itself
Into the sea."

But through the welter of that sad ruin there rang out the clear voice of a philosopher, proclaiming that the only gospel of salvation for Prussia was the gospel of education. At the very moment when French bayonets were in possession of Berlin, Fichte lifted up his voice in the "Reden an die Deutsche Nation," in which, throughout the elaborate argument of fourteen lectures, there was this ever recurring refrain: "Education is the only means by which we can be rescued from our present helpless condition." The keynote of that appeal, the pathetic eloquence of which resounded throughout Germany, was in the sentence: "I hope to convince Germans that nothing but education can rescue us from the miseries that overwhelm us." And the foundation of his argument was laid in a doctrine which he has condensed into a single sentence. "Education," said he, "education, as hitherto conducted by the church, has aimed only at securing for men happiness in another life; but this is not enough, for men need to be taught how to bear themselves in the present life so as to do their duty to the State, to others, and to themselves."
The lectures, which were little else than an eloquent and impassioned elaboration of this theme, made so profound an impression upon the country, and especially upon the Government, that a commission of five of the most eminent scholars of Prussia was appointed to elaborate and recommend a system that would embody these ideas. All grades of education were remodeled and reduced to substantial uniformity of system. To us, in this discussion, it is of chief interest to note that one of the first fruits of the movement was the founding of the university at Berlin; a university which, now that three-quarters of a century have passed, brings annually together, for the most advanced learning the world can give, more than five thousand of the most intelligent and the most aspiring young men of Germany.
It would be easy to point out how the works of such men as Niebuhr and Ranke and Mommsen and Savigny and Boeckh and Virchow and Helmholz, and others of kindred renown, each of whom, in his sphere, has stood at the very pinnacle of human knowledge, have inspired the thoughts and illuminated the paths of scholars in all parts of the world. But, fascinating as this theme would be, it would be more to our purpose to-day to contemplate the effect of this system of education upon the German people and the German nation. It must, however, suffice simply to say that it has taken the shattered and impoverished and disheartened Germany of 1810 and made it the united and prosperous and confident Germany of the present day.
And it was work in some sense akin to this that Washington, our Washington, desired to do for the American people. He saw and deplored certain disintegrating tendencies in education as well as in politics. In the political field, thanks to the efforts chiefly of Hamilton and Marshall and Webster, the thoughts of the country were so led that when the hour of trial came, the tendency was successfully thwarted and the danger, as we now trust, permanently overcome. But there were no Hamiltons or Marshalls or Websters for the work of education. The tongue of history is silent as to what has become of the bequest for a national university embodied in the last will and testament of Washington. Certain it is that the general apathy on the subject was so profound that the means provided for from Washington's private fortune for such a university have never been devoted to the noble purpose for which

they were designed. In striving to live, the country forgot to make provision for living well.

It is perhaps in vain to speculate as to what results would have followed if Washington's plan had been met in the spirit in which it was intended and announced. But it is at least not difficult to imagine that, if the same wisdom had prevailed in organizing our education that characterized our early political history, we should have had an educational center that would have shed its elevating and inspiring influence over the whole country, and, as Washington said, by bringing the youth from all parts of the land together, would have tended, at least, to bind all sections of the country into a more sympathetic and harmonious union.[1]

LXXXIV. The paper of Dr. Andrew D. White, ex-president of Cornell University, published in the Forum for June, 1888, from which the following extracts are taken:

Two or three years since the newspapers announced Mr. Tulane's gift of over a million of dollars to found a university in Louisiana; a little later came Mr. Clarke's gift of two millions, with hints of millions more, to found a university in Massachusetts; and now come details of Governor Stanford's gift of many more millions to found a university in California. During this recent period, too, have come a multitude of noble gifts to strengthen universities already established; among them such as those of Mr. Agassiz, Mr. Greenleaf, and Mr. Boyden, at Harvard; of Mr. Kent, Mr. Marquand, and Mr. Chittenden, at Yale; of Mr. Phœnix, at Columbia; of Mr. Green and Mr. Marquand, at Princeton; of Mr. McCormick, at the University of Virginia; of Mr. Crouse, at Syracuse; of Mr. Sage, Mr. Sibley, and Mr. Barnes, at Cornell, and scores of others.

All these are but the continuation of a stream of munificence which began to flow in the earliest years of the nation, but which has especially swollen since the civil war, in obedience to the thoughts of such as Peabody, Sheffield, Cooper, Cornell, Vassar, Packer, Durant, Sage, Johns Hopkins, Sibley, Case, Rose, and very many more.

Such a tide of generosity bursting forth from the hearts and minds of strong and shrewd men, who differ so widely from each other in residence and ideas, yet flowing in one direction, means something. What is it? At the source of it lies, doubtless, a perception of duty to the country and a feeling of pride in the country's glory. United with this is, naturally, more or less of an honorable personal ambition; but this is not all; strong common sense has done much to create the current and still more to shape its course. For, as to the origin of this stream, the wealthy American knows perfectly that the laws of his country favor the dispersion of inherited wealth rather than its retention; that in two or three generations at most his descendants, no matter how large their inheritance, must come to the level determined by their character and ability; that their character and ability are most likely to be injured, and therefore the level to which they subside lowered, by an inheritance so large as to engender self-indulgence; that while, in Great Britain, the laws and customs of primogeniture and entail enable men of vast wealth to tie up their property, and so to found families, this, in America, is impossible; and that though the tendency to the equalization of fortunes may sometimes be retarded, it can not be prevented.

So, too, as to the direction of the stream; this same common sense has given its main channel. These great donors have recognized the fact that the necessity for universal primary education will always be seen and can be adequately provided for only by the people as a whole; but that the necessity for that advanced education which alone can vivify and energize the whole school system, drawing a rich life up through it, sending a richer life down through it, will rarely be provided for, save by the few men wise enough to understand a great national system of education and strong enough to efficiently aid it.

---

[1] Pp. 17-36.

It is, then, plain, good sense which has led mainly to the development of a munificence such as no other land has seen; therefore it is that the long list of men who have thus distinguished themselves and their country is steadily growing longer, and it may be safely prophesied that the same causes which have led to this large growth of munificence will lead to yet larger growths.

It is in view of these vast future gifts to the country that I present this paper. It is the result of no sudden impulse or whim; it is the outgrowth of years of observation and thought among men as well as among books, in public business as well as in university work, in other countries as well as our own, in other times as well as our own.

Our country has already not far short of four hundred colleges and universities, more or less worthy of those names, besides a vast number of high schools and academies quite as worthy to be called colleges and universities as many which bear those titles. But the system embracing all these has by no means reached its final form. Probably in its more complete development the stronger institutions, to the number of twenty or thirty, will, within a generation or two, become universities in the true sense of the word, restricting themselves to university work, beginning, perhaps, at the studies now usually undertaken in the junior year of our colleges, and carrying them on through the senior year, with two or three years of special or professional work afterwards.

The best of the others will probably accept their mission as colleges in the true sense of the word, beginning the course two years earlier than at present and continuing it to what is now the junior year. Thus they will do a work intermediate between the general school system of the country and the universities, a work which can be properly called collegiate, a work the need of which is now sorely felt, and which is most useful and honorable. Such an organization will give us as good a system as the world has ever seen, probably the best system.

Every man who has thought to much purpose upon this mass of institutions devoted to advanced instruction must feel that it is just now far more important to strengthen those we have than to make any immediate additions to their number. How can this best be done? My answer is that this and a multitude of other needs of the country can be best met by the foundation of a university in the city of Washington.

LXXXV. The contribution by ex-President A. D. White, of New York, to the Forum in January, 1889, wherein he discusses the need of another university:

Down to about twenty-five years ago an American university was a very simple thing indeed. Apart from a few outlying professional departments, it generally consisted of the "college proper," in which the great mass of students was carried, willingly or unwillingly, through the same simple, single course, without the slightest regard for differences between them in aims, tastes, or gifts. * * *

That was probably the lowest point in the history of higher education during the past hundred years. It had not the advantages either of the tutorial system in the English universities or the professorial system in the German universities. Nor had it the advantages of that earlier period in our own country, when strong teachers came directly into living contact with their students, as in the legendary days of Yale, when President Dwight in the chair grappled with Calhoun upon the benches, or of exceptional places later, as when President Hopkins fought over various questions with his student Garfield.

The whole system had become mainly perfunctory. A few students did well in spite of it, but the scholarly energies of most were paralyzed by it. Anything like research or investigation by an undergraduate, in any true sense, was unknown. * * *

Such universities required little endowment. The professors, though frequently men of high character and ability, were few and poorly paid, the salaries being mainly determined by the price at which trustees could fill the faculty with clergymen who had proved unsuccessful as pastors. Money was also saved by requiring one professor to teach many different subjects, his instruction being considered satisfactory if by diligent reading he could keep just ahead of his students. Much money was saved by the employment of tutors, for tutors came cheap. They were, as a rule, young men just out of college, "very poor and very pious," who while studying in the adjacent theological school would, for a small stipend, sit in a box three times a day and "hear recitations." This, as a rule, meant having young men give the words of a text book as nearly as possible, or construe Latin or Greek mainly from the inevitable surreptitious translation, the tutor rarely discussing the subject or making the slightest comment on it, but simply making a mark upon his private book to denote his view of the goodness or badness of each performance.

This was probably the most woeful substitute for education ever devised by the unwisdom of man. Occasionally a bright instructor galvanized an appearance of life into it, but it was dead. A few great men rose above it, but generally the aspirations even of excellent teachers were stifled in the atmosphere it engendered. Cheapest and worst of all were the instructors in modern languages, refugees thrown on our shores by the various European revolutions during the first half of the century; an unkempt race who were willing to submit to the practical jokes of sophomores for wages which would barely keep soul and body together.

As to equipment, all was on the same cheap scale. * * *

Such was the general condition of the leading American universities about the middle of this century. Now, all has been changed; the development in the higher education, even during the last twenty years, in the subjects taught, in the courses presented, in the number of professors, in libraries, laboratories, collections for illustration and research, and in buildings, has been enormous. Institutions for the higher education, when they have been fitly developed toward the proper standard of a university, have been obliged to enlarge their teaching force equipment, and buildings, on very much the same scale of increase seen in our railroads, ocean steamers, hotels, and business generally. * * *

To found an institution and call it a university in these days, with an income of less than a quarter of a million of dollars a year, is a broad farce. Even with that sum many of the most important spheres of university activity must be neglected. Twice the amount is not more than adequate, and Harvard University, which has an income of more than twice that amount, is at this moment showing cogent reasons for demanding more.

And the tendency is ever toward a greater expenditure. This is neither to be scolded at nor whined over. Just as the material demands of this wonderful time have created vast hotels, steamships, and railway systems, so the moral and intellectual demands are creating great universities. One result is as natural and normal as the other; indeed, all are parts of one great demand. To go back from the present universities to the old sort of colleges, would be like giving up railroads and going back to stage coaches. The gentlemen who purpose to meet this demand in education by endowing colleges and universities no better equipped than the best of thirty years ago, are like men who should offer skiffs to persons wishing to cross the Atlantic, or gigs to those wishing to visit California.

To provide and maintain an efficient university library to-day costs more than was required thirty years ago to maintain a large college; to carry on any one of the half dozen laboratories required for a university may cost in these days a sum larger than some of our largest universities then required. * * *

Regarding the advantages of Washington as the seat of a university, the splendid foundations already existing there in men, means, and material, and what might be built on this basis, I shall speak in another article.

LXXXVI. Ex-President A. D. White's discussion of "A University at Washington," in the Forum for February, 1889, from which the following passages are taken:

Regarding the position of Washington as a center in which are brought together great educational resources, and from which are radiated vast influences upon American life, the first main point is, that it is a permanent or temporary residence of very many leading men upon whom a university might draw for its lecture rooms or council chambers. In Congress, from which most people expect little of the sort, are many who can speak with acknowledged authority on subjects which every university worthy of the name has to consider.  *   *   *

Next, as to men specially known in literary pursuits, the veteran historian and statesman who years ago chose Washington as his residence has proved to be a far-sighted pioneer; others have followed him, and the number constantly increases. Everything combines to attract them: the salubrity of the place, save in midsummer, the concourse of men best worth knowing from all parts of the world, and the attractiveness of a city in which intellectual eminence has thus far asserted itself above wealth. So well known is this that the various societies of a literary tendency are more and more making Washington their annual place of meeting; the American Historical Society was one of the first to do this, and others are following its example.

But it is more especially as a source of scientific activity that Washington has taken the foremost place in the nation. It is rapidly becoming one of the great scientific centers of the world. The Smithsonian Institution, the National Museum, the great Government surveys, sundry Government commissions and bureaus whose work is largely scientific, and many retired officers of the Army and Navy who have interested themselves in scientific pursuits, all combine to lay strong foundations for scientific activity.  *   *   *

This aggregation of so many investigators in so many fields has naturally led to the gathering of apparatus and means for carrying on scientific inquiry.  *   *   *

There is no need to dwell upon all the advantages accruing to the country from such an organization; most of them can be easily seen; but I will touch on one which might, at first sight, not be thought of. The city of Washington is rapidly becoming a great metropolis. It is developing the atmosphere which is to give character to the executive, the judicial, and especially the legislative business of the nation.

What shall that atmosphere be? Shall it be made by luxurious millionaires, anxious only for new fields in which to display their wealth? Shall it be an atmosphere of riotous living, without one thought of better things? Shall it be redolent merely of political scheming and stock-jobbing by day and of canvasbacks and terrapin by night? In such a future, legislative cynicism and corruption will be, of course, for they will present the only means by which men can adjust their lungs to the moral atmosphere. Shall it not rather be a capital where, with the higher satisfaction and graces of civilized living, there shall be an atmosphere of thought upon the highest subjects of work in the most worthy fields, of devotion to the noblest aims? Such an atmosphere a great university, with the men and work involved in it, would tend to develop, and in it demagogism would wither and corruption lose the main element of its support. We may well suppose that some considerations of this kind passed through the mind of him whose great name our capital bears, and that they were among the thoughts which prompted him to urge, again and again, the founding there of a university worthy of the nation.

LXXXVII. The significant contribution to the university cause by Mr. Albert Haupert, in a communication of February, 1889, to the Ohio Educational Monthly, from the great University of Berlin, where, like so many others, he had been constrained to seek advantages not to be found in his own country:

"*The main hindrance to literary and scientific progress in the United States is the want of a great central university.*" In this manner did Dr. Döllinger, one of the ablest scholars and theologians in Europe, recently speak before the Munich Academy of Science. I was so struck by the remark that many thoughts about the matter have been awakened by it. The doctor thus not only furnished me with a text, but inspired an entire discourse. * * *

The main weakness of our educational system, as a whole, is its fragmentary, disconnected character. Just herein, then, is the main necessity for establishing a great central national university to be found. Such an institution would at once become the most powerful factor for unity in the entire system, and form the great center for all educational aims and movements. This is what we preëminently need at present—unity in the whole structure, from the humblest schoolroom in the country to the most celebrated university class room—consistency, unity. * * *

Hear what Prof. Lord, of Dartmouth College, says about unity in German schools: "It is impossible that teachers of different grades should be ignorant of the methods and principles that guide each other. *They are all members of one body and work in a common plan.*" In this union lie the strength and superiority of German education.

* * * * * * *

Before concluding this part of the subject I would only emphasize the statement that a great central university would be the most potent general factor for harmonizing the various eccentric movements in our schools, and then we would have removed the reproach which Dr. Döllinger has so justly cast upon us. What have we as a nation to compare with the universities of Berlin, Oxford, or Vienna? We could secure a combination of talent which would become the pride of the nation and rival the greatest seats of learning in Europe. Then so many American students would not be compelled to go to Europe because they are not satisfied with the attainments of the average student at home. This institution is bound to come into existence sooner or later, and I am surprised that our Government, whose generous heart is so ready to respond to the welfare of the people, has not taken steps with regard to the matter. * * * Then our educational system, like the great solar system, would have a sun and a center of gravity, around which all the planets and their satellites would revolve in unity and unbroken harmony.[1]

LXXXVIII. The address of Prof. Herbert B. Adams, of Johns Hopkins University, before the National Educational Association, at a meeting in Washington, March, 1889:

It is needless to give further illustrations of State aid to American universities. * * * The principle of State aid to at least one leading institution in each Commonwealth is established in every one of the Southern and Western States. * * * Turning now from historic examples of State aid to the higher education by individual American Commonwealths, let us inquire briefly concerning the attitude of the United States Government towards institutions of science and sound learning.

Washington's grand thought of a national university, based upon individual endowment, may be found in many of his writings, but the clearest and strongest statement occurs in his last will and testament. There he employed the following significant language: [Quoted already, on p. 41.]

* * * * * * *

Here was the individual foundation of a national university. Here was the first suggestion of that noble line of public policy subsequently adopted in 1846 by our

[1] Ohio Educational Monthly, Vol. 30, pp. 193-196.

General Government in relation to the Smithsonian Institution. The will of James Smithson, of England, made in 1826, was "to found at Washington, under the name of the Smithsonian Institution, an establishment for the increase and diffusion of knowledge among men." A simpler educational bequest, with such far-reaching results, was never before made. Whether James Smithson was influenced to this foundation by the example of Washington is a curious problem. Smithson's original bequest, amounting to something over $500,000, was accepted by Congress for the purpose designated, and was placed in the Treasury of the United States, where by good administration and small additional legacies (in two cases from other individuals) the sum has increased to over $700,000. Besides this, the Smithsonian Institution now has a library equal in value to the original endowment, and acquired by the simple process of government exchanges, and it owns buildings equal in value to more than half the original endowment. During the past year, as shown by the Secretary's report, the Institution was "charged by Congress with the care and disbursement of sundry appropriations," amounting to $220,000. The National Museum is under the direction of the Secretary of the Smithsonian, and the Government appropriations to that Museum since its foundation aggregate nearly $2,000,000. The existence and ever-increasing prosperity of the Smithsonian Institution are standing proofs that private foundations may receive the fostering care of Government without injurious results.

George Washington, like James Smithson, placed a private bequest, so that the General Government might extend to it "a favoring hand;" but in those early days Congress had no conception of the duties of Government towards education and science, although attention was repeatedly called to these subjects by enlightened executives like Thomas Jefferson, "Father of the University of Virginia," James Madison, James Monroe, and John Quincy Adams. It took Congress ten years to establish the Smithsonian Institution after the bequest had been accepted and the money received. Unfortunately, George Washington's Potomac stock never paid but one dividend, and there was no pressure in those days towards educational appropriations from an ever-increasing surplus. The affairs of the Potomac Company were finally merged into the Chesapeake and Ohio Canal, which became a profitable enterprise, and endures to this day. What became of George Washington's "consolidated stock" of that period, history does not record. Jared Sparks, Washington's biographer, thought the stock was "held in trust" by the new company for the destined university. There is probably little danger that it will ever be thrown upon the market in a solid block by the Treasury of the United States, to which the stock legally belongs, unless the present surplus should suddenly vanish, and the General Government be forced to realize upon its assets for the expenses of the administration. * * *

Washington's dream of a great university, rising grandly upon the Maryland bank of the Potomac, has remained a dream for more than a century. But there is nothing more real or persistent than the dreams of great men, whether statesmen like Baron von Stein, or poets like Dante and Petrarch, or prophets like Savonarola, or thinkers like St. Thomas Aquinas, the fathers of the church and of Greek philosophy. States are overthrown; literatures are lost; temples are destroyed; systems of thought are shattered to pieces like the statues of Phidias; but somehow truth and beauty, art and architecture, forms of poetry, ideals of liberty and government, of sound learning and of the education of youth, these immortal dreams are revived from age to age and take concrete shape before the very eyes of successive generations.[1]

LXXXIX. Support of the proposition by Dr. Otis T. Mason, curator of the ethnological department of the National Museum—

[1] Proceedings Nat. Ed. Ass'n, 1889, pp. 267–270.

(1) In a communication of 1889, to the president and trustees of Columbian University, from which the following, quoted by Dr. J. C. Welling in his published paper hereinafter mentioned:

In the first place, such an institution would draw students from all parts of the land, and instead of impoverishing the State institutions would only stimulate them.

Secondly, an increased local patronage might be expected from Maryland and Virginia, but this increment would be small so far as it is determined by geographical considerations alone.

Thirdly, and preëminently, all who have written about this subject seem to have entirely overlooked a principal source of supply in the immediate vicinage of such a university. I refer to the Government employés. There are not far from 10,000 clerks in our Washington civil list, 2,000 of whom, it may be estimated, are anxious for university instruction of some kind; but let us say 1,000. Already in the Columbian, Georgetown, Howard, and other law and medical schools of Washington, we find 500 persons earning a living by working for the Government, and at the same time pursuing professional studies. The National Museum, the Geological Survey, the Patent Office, etc., are thronged with young men—some of them graduated from our State colleges—who would be glad to pursue university studies.

I have given much thought to this subject, and there is scarcely a month in which I am not importuned for special instruction which now can not be had short of Baltimore, in the Johns Hopkins University.[1]

(2) By his lecture before the historical seminary of Johns Hopkins University on the Educational Aspect of the United States National Museum, from which these quotations are made:

The interpretation of Smithson's bequest, elaborated by the four men whose names I have mentioned—Henry, Baird, Goode, and Langley—makes our Institution a great world university in the highest sense of the word *universitas*. The increase and diffusion of knowledge to all men so far as in us lies, the increase of knowledge by the exploration of the heavens, the earth, and the waters for new knowledge of all and every kind, and the diffusion of knowledge by communicating to all the researches of all which last is only another name for increase by diffusion. The Smithsonian Institution has come to be a world university for the increase of knowledge, first, by research; second, by publication; third, by the international exchange, which I may be permitted to explain at a little more length.

For the increase of knowledge among men, the Smithsonian Institution has international exchange, its publications, its library, its bureau of ethnology and other explorations, and its museum.

By the international exchange it is the aim of our Institution to put its publications and those of the Government into every great library of the world, to place its monographs into the hands of every specialist in the world, to afford a central office through which every explorer for knowledge may speak to every other explorer of knowledge, without money and without price.[2] * * *

By the elaboration of these several points the author makes a showing not only of the marvelous achievements of the Smithsonian Institution, but also of the instrumentalities and agencies directed by its officers

[1] The Columbian University: Notes on its relation to the city of Washington considered as the seat of a national university, p. 16.

[2] Notes supplementary to the Johns Hopkins University, Studies in Historical and Political Science, 1890, No. 4.

and staff of scientists, that more than justifies the already accepted theory of their practical availability and incalculable value as constituent or coördinate parts of the proposed national university.

XC. Support of the general proposition by President James C. Welling, in the publication of June, 1889, entitled "The Columbian University: Notes on its relations to the City of Washington considered as the seat of a National University;" from which are quoted the following passages, to wit:

Suffice it to say, that the Government of the United States makes an annual appropriation of nearly $3,000,000 for the support of scientific work which, in its several departments, has its headquarters in Washington. * * * A university founded here might immediately profit by the fruits of that vast expenditure.

But, in studying the intellectual resources of Washington in connection with the possibilities of a great university, it is not enough to consider the educational plant here provided, and the eminent masters of science here congregated, but we must also consider the special constituency from which such a university might hope to draw its patrons and pupils.

Washington is to-day a great educational center, not simply because it is a great political center, and not simply because it has become since the civil war a brilliant social center, but because it has become the great scientific center of the whole country, and is the favorite meeting place of learned societies, many of which gather in Washington from all quarters of the land for an annual exchange of discussions and ideas. When Prof. John Tyndall was delivering in Washington, some years ago, his course of popular lectures on light, he remarked to me that he knew of no city in Europe which could gather a congregation of scientific workers and original investigators so large as that which he then met in The Philosophical Society of Washington, under the presidency of Joseph Henry. This society, the oldest of its kind in Washington is only one of the scientific bodies which surround that parent organization at the present time. * * *

It remains to say that all these great centers of scientific study and activity are surmounted, sustained, and replenished by the best and largest collection of books in the whole country. This collection consists not only of the library of Congress, the largest single collection in the land, but is also supplemented by important special libraries connected with each of the great Departments of the General Government, and with each of the several bureaus among which the scientific work of the Government is here distributed. Every branch of human knowledge has a literary deposit in Washington. For instance, under the head of science alone, the Smithsonian Institution has a deposit reckoned by more than 250,000 titles in the alcoves of the library of Congress. In law the same library comprises an invaluable collection of more than 50,000 volumes, covering the jurisprudence of the civilized world. We thus have in the city of Washington more than a million of volumes, selected by experts in the several departments of knowledge, and so housed and administered in close juxtaposition that they are easily accessible to students, whether for reference, for comparative research, or for careful reading; and all this without money and without price on the part of the university or its pupils. How large a saving of university funds may be effected under this head in Washington can be inferred when I recall the fact that the Congress of the United States has just made an appropriation of $6,000,000 for the proper preservation of the literary treasures of the Government in a national library building to be erected almost under the eaves of the National Capitol.

In the Corcoran Gallery of Art, the most richly endowed institution of its kind in the country (it has a free endowment of $1,000,000), provision is also made among us for the study of the fine arts. Free instruction in drawing and painting is given in the art school of this gallery.

To show how all these appliances may be made directly tributary to university studies with a vast saving of expense on the score of university administration, let me take one or two illustrative examples—say, the National Museum and the chemical bureaus of Washington.

The National Museum has twenty-two distinct scientific departments under its jurisdiction: The departments of comparative anatomy, of mammals, of birds, of reptiles, of fishes, of mollusks, of insects, of marine invertebrates, of plants, of fossil vertebrates, of paleozoic fossil invertebrates, of mesozoic fossil invertebrates, of cenozoic fossil invertebrates, of fossil plants, of geology and petrology, of mineralogy, of metallurgy and mining, of prehistoric archæology, of ethnology, of oriental antiquities, of American aboriginal pottery, of arts and industries, comprising under these last-named heads numismatics, graphic arts, foods, textiles, fisheries, historical relics, materia medica, naval architecture, history of transportation, etc.

Each of these departments is placed under a curator, and is provided with the necessary appliances for original research; and these appliances are yearly increasing in completeness and efficiency. In addition to these special appliances each curator has his laboratory with its necessary apparatus, his working library, and his study-series of specimens for use in original investigation. In connection with his sectional library each curator has access to the central library of the museum, now containing over 20,000 volumes, as also to the library of Congress. These scientific laboratories are always open to students and investigators who come either to observe methods of work or to pursue researches of their own with the aid of these appliances. It should be added, as bearing directly on the problem of university education, that each of these departmental libraries and laboratories is of the kind which a university would require if it has a specialist of its own engaged in a minute subdivision of science corresponding to that of the Museum. Some of these laboratories, notably those of zoölogy, geology, and botany, have a fuller outfit than those of any American university, while others of these laboratories have no analogues at all in the best equipped of our educational institutions. Prof. Otis T. Mason, so honorably known to the scientific world as one of the learned curators of the National Museum, can authenticate all that I have said concerning the possible relations which this great scientific workshop is actually bearing, and can be made to bear, to the cause of university education. * * *

*        *        *        *        *        *        *

But, it may be said, what relation has all this affluence of scientific apparatus to the special behoof of a great university in Washington? I answer, much every way. A very large part of the sum required for the establishment of a university at Cambridge, at New Haven, and at Princeton must needs be expended for what is technically called "the educational plant"—buildings, books, costly apparatus, specimens, collections in zoölogy, botany, archæology, etc. And then large sums must be annually expended for the preservation and administration of these buildings and of these illustrative materials. The necessary expenditures of this kind are reduced to a minimum at Washington, for here the choicest materials of education already exist under the custody of the Government, and are offered ready-made to the hands of the university which is able to wield them in its service. Nor is this all. In connection with these scientific departments may be found very many of the foremost men of science in our country, and (in certain specialties) in the whole world. I need but call the names of Newcomb, of Maj. Powell, of Asaph Hall, of Langley, of G. Brown Goode, of Dr. John S. Billings, and of many others to set this fact in a clear light. * * *

Such a university as I here prefigure would come in no rivalry with any existing institution under the control of any denomination. It would aim to be the crown and culmination of our State institutions, borrowing graduates from them and repaying its debt by contributing to them in turn the inspiration of high educational standards, and helping also in its measure to train the experts in theology, law, medicine, science, philosophy, and letters, who should elsewhere strive to keep alive the traditions of a progressive scholarship under the auspices of Christianity. It is not enough that our colleges should perpetuate and transmit the existing sum of human knowledge. We must also have our workers on the boundaries of a progressive knowledge, if we are to establish our hold on the directive forces of modern society. We must have our men who can work effectively for the increase of learning, because they stand in this living age of ours on the summit of the world's actual achievements in every branch of human thought and inquiry.

Let us now turn to consider, for a moment, the opportunities which Washington offers for the study of chemical science—that science which to-day is transforming in so many aspects the private and the public economy of the world. There are at least seven centers of chemical activity conducted under the auspices of the Government at the national capital.[1]

XCI. Support of the proposition by Superintendent William A. Mowry, of Salem, Massachusetts, in a paper read before the National Educational Association, at Nashville, in 1889, which paper, entitled "A National University, a Study," emphatically declares:

The success of Johns Hopkins University has been phenomenal. It gives opportunities for a higher standard of scholarship than we before possessed. It has helped to elevate the work of all the colleges, but it has also served to show clearly the necessity of still further advances. What is needed now is an institution far beyond Johns Hopkins. The liberality of wealthy Americans has been so great as almost to make it seem that it had no limit, but it certainly is not without limit. It can hardly be expected that private munificence will be able to establish a university in this country with sufficient means to perform adequately the service required in the higher realms of learning. We are, therefore, shut up to the necessity of having this needed institution established by the whole people as represented by our National Government. That, and that alone, will be able to accomplish this great work.

Again,

I do not think there could be found sufficient reasons for establishing by the Government a national college of the ordinary type. The State universities and the large number of colleges established in the several States by private munificence are sufficient for the needs of the people. If the proposed national university were to be modeled after the plan of Harvard or Yale, Cornell or Ann Arbor, or even Johns Hopkins, it had better not be founded. The purpose and scope of such an institution should be for higher and broader work than can now be done in any existing institution. Its object should be largely for original investigation. It should, in many departments, at least, aim primarily to reach out to the unknown. Its standard should be higher than that of any institution in the world.

And again:

The United States should be not only the greatest and strongest of the nations, but should be the wisest and most beneficent. She has laid a broad foundation for a pyramid (which should be larger and more enduring than those of Egypt) in the general diffusion of the elements of learning for all her youth in our beneficent system of public schools. Let her now, by the establishment of this national university, build securely and strongly upon this basis, and extend upward this great pyramid till its apex shall be high up in the heavens, above all mists of ignorance, superstition, vice, and crime.[2]

---

[1] pp. 7, 16.   [2] Proceedings Nat. Ed. Ass'n. 1889, pp. 189-202.

XCII. Support of the main proposition by Rev. Dr. George D. Boardman, of Philadelphia, in a leaflet of October 30, 1889, entitled "An American University at Washington," in which occurs the following:

Let me mention a few reasons why, as it seems to me, the city of Washington is the best place for the proposed university:

First. Washington is already the capital of our country. As such it is neutral ground for our whole nation, the common property of the North, South, East, West. If our national university is planted at Washington no one can complain of sectional partiality.

Again, Washington is not only the civic capital of our Union, it is also our scientific capital, and bids to be our intellectual center. Recall its magnificent educational appliances, for example, the Smithsonian Institution, the National Museum, the Geological Survey, the Bureau of Ethnology, the Patent Office, the Army Medical Museum, the Naval Museum of Hygiene, the Weather Bureau, the Coast Survey, the Bureau of Hydrography, the National Observatory, the Agricultural Department, the Botanical Garden, the Zoölogical Garden, the Department of Education, the Corcoran Gallery of Art, the Anthropological Society, the Biological Society, the Botanical Society, the Chemical Society, the Geographical Society, the Historical Association, the Mathematical Society, the Philosophical Society, etc., bringing together a national body of some 600 eminent experts; in fact, nearly all the leading scientific bodies of our country now hold their annual meetings at Washington. Recall also the magnificent libraries of Washington, containing more than a million volumes, on every variety of subject, open to every inquirer. All these, with educational opportunities, and many others, already exist at Washington and could hardly be duplicated except at cost of many years of toil and many millions of money.

Again, Washington is becoming more and more the winter home of cultivated, opulent families, thus rapidly taking rank as one of the social centers of the United States. President White, Senator Hawley, and others in recent contributions to our periodical literature, have pointed out the preëminent advantages of Washington, as the university city of America. In brief, Washington is largely, so to speak, the nation's sensorium—the point where the nation's impressions are received, and whence the nation's conclusions are distributed.

Having in another portion of this paper made room for an outline of the movement of 1849–'52 for the establishment of a "national university" at Albany, notwithstanding the fact that it was not in pursuance of the plan originated by Washington and supported by the long line of its advocates from his day to the present, and, more than anything, because such movement gave evidence of the yearning desire of that day; so now, after just forty years of national growth and the multiplication of institutions broader, higher, and better equipped than any in that day, mention is here made of new enterprises, with similar ends in view, lately begun by two of the great churches of America.

The Catholic University of America, incorporated in 1886, and thus begun but yesterday, was inaugurated with imposing ceremonies, on November 13, 1889. The event is thus briefly chronicled in the official report of that date:

The first centenary of the hierarchy in the United States was fittingly crowned by the inauguration of the Catholic University of America. Our Holy Father, Pope Leo XIII, in his apostolic letter of March 7, 1889, notes the relation between these two events. "In this matter," he says, "we deem most worthy of all praise your intention of inaugurating the university during the centenary of the establishment of the Ecclesiastical Hierarchy in your country, as a monument and perpetual memorial of that most auspicious event."

The happy coincidence thus alluded to by his Holiness was an incentive which principally spurred on the work of preparation and secured its accomplishment in due time. An army of workmen were engaged on the building [for the theological department] up to the very eve of the dedication; but when the eventful day dawned all was in readiness. The structure was richly and tastefully decorated from ground floor to roof. The chapel, with its thirteen altars, was exquisitely adorned. The professors and most of the students were already lodged in their apartments, ready to receive and welcome the host of expected guests.

The twofold object of this institution is set forth in a spirit of candor and courage. It is to be not only a university, but a *Catholic* university. As such it sends its greetings to all Christendom, and also sets forth its claims to the confidence of lovers of truth everywhere, irrespective of church or creed. That its purposes may be duly represented, we quote the following passages from the formal discourses of those who had part in the inauguration.

From the sermon delivered by the Rt. Rev. R. Gilmour, bishop of Cleveland:

Civilization is limited only by education. The civilization of this nineteenth century is but the accumulated results of the world's history. The serpent tempted Eve with the offer of knowledge, and the limit was: "Ye shall be as gods, knowing good and evil." * * *

The motive that has brought here to-day the Chief Magistrate of this great Republic and these high dignitaries of church and state, and this distinguished audience of the laity, is worthy of deepest thought. Kind friends! you are not here to assist at the dedication of this fair building—classic in its lights and shades of art—to the mere cultivation of the arts and sciences, valuable though they are. A higher motive has brought you here, and a higher motive prompted the first munificent gift and subsequent generosity that have rendered this institution possible. This building has just been blessed and forever dedicated to the cultivation of the science of sciences—the knowledge of God. It was well to have begun with the Divinity department, if for nothing else than to teach that all true education must begin in God and find its truth and direction in God. * * *

There is a widespread mistake, a rapidly growing political and social heresy, which assumes and asserts that the state is all temporal and religion all spiritual. This is not only a doctrinal heresy, but if acted on would end in ruin to both spiritual and temporal. No more can the state exist without religion than can the body exist without the soul, and no more can religion exist without the state, and, on earth, carry on its work, than can the soul, on earth, without the body, do its work. * *

The morality of the citizen is the real strength of the state, but the teaching of morality is the function of religion, and in so much is religion necessary to the state.

* * *

In the light of the above fundamental all-important truths, it is not difficult to see how valuable Christian education is to society. Education refines society, elevates man, and directs all to the higher good. No nobler mission than that of a teacher; by office a leader, by talent an inventor, and by genius an originator and director of power.

Gioja of Amalfi gave the mariner's compass; Columbus, America; Watt, the steam engine; and Morse, the telegraph; and these four men have revolutionized the material world. The single thought, "No man shall be oppressed for conscience and that other thought, "All men are created equal", has given a continent its political faith.

Now, in the light of these grave and fundamental truths the question naturally arises, "What are the end and scope of a University?"—a question that will be answered according as we understand the end and mission of the education. * * *

The end, then, of a university is to gather within its walls the few who are brighter in intellect and keener in thought, and to expand and vivify within them knowledge; then send them forth leaders to instruct and train the masses. * * *

The tendency of the age is to level down; to make smatterers instead of thinkers. Perhaps not since the days of Plato and Cicero has there been less depth of thought than at present. Education has increased in quantity, but lessened in quality. * * * To break away from the past is the monomania of the day, and he who does that most recklessly is the Star in the East. Amid this general leveling down and breaking away we have but faint echoes and fewer voices standing for the truth or giving sturdy blows to error. * * * Much has been done, much is doing; but much remains to be done to train the few to be leaders. * * *

In the curriculum of this Catholic University the best in each of the several branches will be adopted, and in the light of European and American experience improved upon. * * * Let the great ambition of this university be to lead in all that tends to elevate our race, benefit our fellow-citizens, and bless our country.

From the discourse of Rev. Father Fidelis on "The Vitality of the Church a Manifestation of God":

The work which the Catholic Church has accomplished in this country during the century which we are bringing to a close is the same which she has done in other ages and in other lands, but she has done it in a new way, and in her own way. She has taken hold of new conditions of things and adapted herself to them; and the result of her work is a structure distinctive and typical of the age and country in which we live, and differing from anything that has preceded it as truly as the church of the middle ages differed from the church of the fathers. And, mind you—for this is the point of all my discourse—she has done this not by any prudence of human forethought, not by any cunning adaptation of policy, but simply because she s a living force, capable of acting in all time and in all places, so that she has become American without ceasing for an instant to be Catholic. * * *

Therefore, in inaugurating to-day the work of this American Catholic University we feel that we are the privileged agents of God in carrying on the operations of His holy church. If you have read history, however slightly, you know, my friends, that the great universities of Christendom were Catholic in their origin. Long before the outbreak of the sixteenth century, the old cathedral and monastic schools had developed into seats of learning which dotted every land until the youth of Europe grew into an army of scholastic enthusiasts. Well, therefore, may we feel that in what we behold accomplished this day there is nothing forced, or rash, or immature. Surely the time has come for such a work, and surely it was fitting that the church in America should crown her first century of progress by calling into existence an institution which indicates once more her claim to an undying vitality. The days of darkness are over. The long winter of poverty and struggle is ended. A brighter era has dawned at last. "Arise, shine, O Jerusalem, for thy light is come, and the glory of the Lord has arisen upon thee!"

It is proper to add that the university thus inaugurated has a magnificent location upon a sufficient tract of land in a commanding suburb of Washington, adjoining the Soldiers' Home; that besides its divinity school, whose building is one of the finest in America, other departments are being provided for by the erection of costly edifices, and that the institution already rests upon a very considerable pecuniary foundation.

XCIII. The approval of the Nation, whose editor, in discussing the Edmunds bill of recent date, said in the issue of December 12, 1889:

It may be laid down as a rule that no real university can exist which is not governed by the faculty. A university at Washington so governed might be the glory of this country, for the riches of Washington in libraries and scientific collections [it might have added scientific men] are now extraordinarily great.

XCIV. The incidental service of Dr. Frank W. Blackmar, some time Fellow in Johns Hopkins University and now professor in the State University of Kansas, by his recent History of Federal and State Aid to Higher Education, published in 1890 by the Bureau of Education; in which report, while mentioning the attempts to found a national university, he likewise sets forth the manner in which Congress, by appropriations of land and money during a period of more than a hundred years, has helped to build up many collegiate institutions in all parts of the United States, thus establishing forever the principle on which the university proposition rests, and in effect showing that it but remains to the Government to crown and complete the work thus wisely begun by supplying that final institution, which the individual States can not provide, and yet which alone can harmonize and complete the higher education in America.

From this valuable document one gleans, among others, the following items of land and money appropriations:

(1) Lands by the township, under acts of 1787 and 1800, amounting to over one million acres, for the support of State universities.

(2) A considerable but unascertained proportion of the money surplus of twenty-eight millions dollars distributed to the States in 1836 and never recalled.

(3) A portion of the three and a half millions dollars constituting the share of education in the total proceeds of land sales under the percentage acts of 1841 and later.

(4) A portion of the three and a half millions acres accorded by different States to education out of the nine and a half millions acres given by Congress in 1841 for internal improvements.

(5) Further important sums not definitely known, from the sale of over fifty millions acres of swamp lands disposed of under provisions of the act of 1850, from which source alone the University of California is said to have derived important aid.

(6) Revenues in a number of States from the sale of saline lands, with appropriations thereof to the support of colleges of agriculture and the mechanic arts.

(7) The more than $15,000,000 already derived from the lands accorded to States by the act of July 2, 1862, for the support of colleges and the mechanic arts; which grant has resulted not only in the establishment of many important technical institutions, but also at the same time in such strengthening of the State universities that some of them are thus early taking their places in the foreground of the great university field.

(8) The appropriation by act of March 2, 1887, of $15,000 per annum to each State for experimental purposes in aid of scientific agriculture in the broadest sense of that term, a yet further incidental reënforcement of the many State universities.

(9) The aggregate of over $20,000,000 appropriated for the support of the Military Academy at West Point and the Naval Academy at Annapolis.

(10) The establishment, equipment, and support of the Naval Observatory and the purely scientific bureaus of the Government at Washington.

(11) The large sums of money appropriated for the convenience and support of the Congressional and departmental libraries.

(12) The hundreds of thousands expended in buildings for the scientific museums of the Government, and the more than $3,000,000 a year so wisely granted for their support.

XCV. The support of this proposition by Dr. G. Brown Goode, assistant secretary of the Smithsonian Institution and director of the National Museum, in papers contributed by him to the American Historical Association and afterwards (1890) republished under title of "The Origin of the National Scientific and Educational Institutions of the United States"; also by his earnest and effective efforts to so plan and develop the National Museum as to increase its general educational value to the utmost, and thus the better fit it to become an important coöperative agency when the National University shall have been established. [To the work of Dr. Goode this paper is indebted for a number of facts of interest, and especially for an account of the university efforts of Samuel Blodget, Richard Rush, and Minister Barlow.]

XCVI. The approval of the New York Times, March 10, 1890:

An institution that would strengthen our whole educational system. * * * The subject of a national university endowed and supported, in part at least, by the National Government has been discussed by prominent educators throughout the United States.

When the ambitious student has completed his college course he finds himself only at the outskirts of the field of knowledge, and if his ambition still speeds him on he is obliged to go abroad to complete his education.

The impression has gone abroad that the American colleges are opposed to the establishment of a national university. In order to ascertain the truth of this report a representative of the Times interviewed many of the professors of Cornell University and found them heartily in favor of a national university, provided it should be organized on a sufficiently broad basis. * * * The opinions of the entire university are epitomized in the following interviews with President Adams and ex-President Andrew D. White. [Views set forth in other portions of this paper.]

XCVII. "A bill to establish the University of the United States," introduced in the Senate of the United States, on May 14, 1890, by Senator George F. Edmunds, of Vermont.

Following is the record of proceedings of that date on this subject:

Mr. Edmunds introduced a bill (S. 3822) to establish the University of the United States; which was read twice by its title.

Mr. EDMUNDS. This is a special and peculiar subject. This bill is a rough draft I made when I was not well, and it may not be at all perfect. I have introduced it in order that the subject may be considered; and as it is a special and peculiar subject, with the assent of my friend, the chairman of the Committee on Education and Labor, I move that it be referred to a select committee of nine.

The VICE-PRESIDENT. It will be so referred in the absence of objection.[1]

The general provisions of said bill are as follows:

The corporation to consist of a board of regents, composed of the President of the United States, the several members of the President's Cabinet, the Chief Justice of

---

[1] Annals, Fifty-first Cong., 1st sess., p. 4643.

the United States, and twelve citizens of the United States, no two of whom shall be residents of the same State, who shall be appointed by a concurrent resolution of the two Houses of Congress. Vacancies occurring to be filled in like manner. The full term of the members chosen to be nine years, and the division to be in three classes, whose members shall at first severally hold for three, six, and nine years, respectively.

The institution to do post-graduate work and to be also devoted to the advancement of knowledge by means of researches and investigations.

The board of regents to have authority to create such offices, and to establish and support such professorships, fellowships, scholarships, and courses of instruction as they may think proper, and to make proper regulations for the government of the institution.

The first meeting of the regents to be called by the President of the United States. The regents to make a complete statement of the affairs and transactions of the institution annually.

The regents to have authority to secure the necessary ground and provide the requisite buildings, as well as to fix the compensation of all persons employed in whatever capacity.

The sum of $500,000 is appropriated for the purchase of grounds and the erection of buildings.

The sum of $5,000,000 is set apart in the Treasury of the United States as a perpetual fund, bearing interest at 4 per cent per annum for the support and maintenance of the university.

The regents are authorized to receive donations in aid of the institution; which must be applied as directed by the donor.

No special sectarian belief or doctrine to be taught or promoted in the institution; but the study and consideration of Christian theology not to be excluded.

No person otherwise eligible to be denied the privileges of the university on account of race, color, citizenship, or religious belief.

XCVIII. The creation, by the Senate, of the select committee to establish the University of the United States, June 4, 1890, and the appointment thereon of George F. Edmunds, chairman, and Senators Sherman, Ingalls, Blair, Dolph, Harris, Butler, Gibson, and Barbour.

XCIX. The pamphlet of Prof. B. A. Hinsdale, of Michigan University, entitled "Topics in the Educational History of the United States", published in 1890, in which, without very positively committing himself to the enterprise of securing the establishment of a national university, he furnishes interesting facts in the history of the subject, with such comments upon the attitudes of the early Presidents as clearly indicate the trend of his opinion:

The facts as cited suggest some reflections. First, it is apparent that the national university idea attracted considerable attention when our present Government was in process of establishment. It seems, in fact, to have been quite commonly assumed that such an institution would be established when the fitting time came. Some may read between the lines that small, provincial ideas prevailed a century ago. Not only Washington's ideas, but also Jefferson's, may appear strangely inadequate as respects ways and means. But we must remember that the whole scale of things has increased enormously in one hundred years, and that ideas then large are to-day small.

## Concerning President John Adams:

The first President Adams was in thorough sympathy with all reasonable efforts to advance learning and science. His writings abound in interesting passages relating to the subject of education. Nor was he restrained from urging a national university by any constitutional theories. * * *

Adams's administration was a troubled one; and he may have been restrained by a conviction that no mere recommendation of his on such a matter would avail. He was too familiar with the ill-success that had attended Washington's efforts, although they were enforced by a proffered endowment. Besides, his addresses to Congress were brief and his recommendations few in number.

C. "A bill (H. R. 10816) to establish a memorial national university," introduced in the House of Representatives of the United States on June 7, 1890, by Mr. O'Neill, of Pennsylvania, by request. The preamble:

Whereas the Government of the United States of America has inaugurated a celebration of the four hundredth anniversary of the discovery of America by Christopher Columbus, to be held in the year 1893; and,

Whereas it is proper that some permanent memorial of that great event should be erected at the capital of the nation; and,

Whereas the experiment of a free republic with a constitutional form of government and an indissoluble union of States has been demonstrated in the first hundred years of its existence to be practicable and successful, and the principles of political freedom, equality, and justice have been guaranteed to all its citizens; and,

Whereas the perpetuity of the Government and the guaranties of its Constitution are dependent on the virtue, intelligence, and patriotism of the people:

Therefore, in order to the promotion of the broadest culture in literature, science, art, ethics, and political economy among the people, and as a light-bearer to all nations of the principles of constitutional liberty upon which this Government is established,

*Be it enacted,* * * * That a university is hereby established in the District of Columbia, to be called the American University.

The constitution of the board of curators of the American University is left blank. It is to have the usual powers.

All moneys donated or devised as permanent funds to be principal, and as the same accrues to be invested in United States bonds, which shall remain forever intact, although subject, as necessity may demand, to investment and reinvestment in bonds of the United States so long as available.

The board of curators to consist of 21 members; the President and Vice-President of the United States, the Chief Justice, the Secretary of State, the Secretary of the Treasury, the Attorney-General, the Secretary of the Smithsonian Institution, the Director of the Geological Survey, and the Superintendent of the Naval Observatory to be *ex officio* members.

All vacancies in the board to be filled by a vote of a majority of all its members at the annual meetings thereof, and all vacancies after the year 1900 to be filled from the rolls of the alumni of the university. Any donor whose gift amounts to $100,000 to be eligible as a member of the board.

No sectarian or antireligious belief to be inculcated in the institution.

Free scholarship, under proper restriction, to be in time accorded to applicants from the several Congressional districts, to alumni of existing colleges and universities, and to each of the Pan-American Republics.

All members of the university to have access without charge to all libraries, museums, lectures, and other sources of information controlled by the Government.

No person otherwise eligible for admission to be excluded on account of sex, race, color, citizenship, or religious belief.

As a means of carrying this plan into effect, the sum of $500,000 to be appropriated for grounds and buildings, and the further sum of $1,000,000 annually for the period of ten years for the permanent endowment of the institution; the same to be invested in bonds of the United States, bearing 4 per cent interest, payable quarterly.

CI. The action of the Senate of the United States on December 17, 1890, upon motion of Senator Cullom, in continuing the Select Committee to Establish the University of the United States during the Fifty-second Congress:

Mr. Cullom submitted the following resolution; which was considered by unanimous consent and agreed to:

*Resolved*, That the following constitute the Select Committees of the Senate of the United States, for the Fifty-second Congress: * * *

To establish the University of the United States[1]

[By virtue of this action the university committee consists at present of the following Senators. Redfield Proctor, of Vermont, chairman; John Sherman, of Ohio; Joseph N. Dolph, of Oregon; William D. Washburn, of Minnesota; Watson C. Squire, of Washington; Matthew C. Butler, of South Carolina; Randall L. Gibson, of Louisiana; John S. Barbour, of Virginia;[2] James H. Kyle, of South Dakota.]

CII. The unanimous action of the Senate on March 2, 1891, in further continuing the aforesaid Select Committee to Establish the University of the United States, as appears by the following record:

Mr. Edmunds. I ask unanimous consent to move that the select committee appointed to consider Senate bill 3822, of the first session of this Congress, to establish a university of the United States, may be continued until the end of the next session. I wish to say, in asking this unanimous consent, that, owing to the stress of revenue matters in the last season and other matters in this, I have not been able, as the chairman of that committee, to find myself justified in even calling the committee together, important as this measure is. The committee has not had clerk, or messenger, or stenographer, and does not propose to have. Therefore, the request I make will not involve any expense to the United States; but I hope that the members of the committee may be able before the end of the next session of Congress to report one way or the other upon this subject of national importance.

The Presiding Officer (Mr. Platt in the chair). The Senator from Vermont asks unanimous consent that the select committee consider the bill (S. 3822) to establish the university of the United States, be authorized to continue its sessions during the recess of the Congress, and during the next session. Is there objection? The Chair hears none, and it is so ordered.[3]

CIII. The paper entitled "A National University, its Character and Purpose," read August 20, 1891, by Lester F. Ward, before Section I of the American Association for the Advancement of Science, at its annual meeting in Washington, D. C.[4]

---

[1] Cong. Record, 52d Cong., 1st. sess., p. 85.
[2] Deceased.
[3] Annals, 51st Cong., 2d sess., p. 3656.
[4] *Science*, Vol. xviii, p. 28.

For the same general reason which justifies incidental allusion in this record to the Albany and Catholic enterprises of 1852 and 1886–89, mention may be made in this place of the more recent university efforts of the Methodist Episcopal Church. Moved, as it would seem, by considerations pertaining to the educational needs of the country, the accumulation of facilities at Washington, and the special interests of that particular religious denomination, the Methodists of the country, under lead of Bishop John F. Hurst, in 1891 inaugurated a movement like that of the Catholic Church above referred to, and have since been actively engaged in forwarding the enterprise of establishing a great Methodist university at the National Capital.

The incorporation was effected on May 28, 1891. Omitting the names of trustees, the charter of the proposed institution reads as follows:

*Know all men by these presents,* That the undersigned, citizens of the United States, desiring to associate ourselves and to become incorporated in order to establish and maintain in the District of Columbia, under the auspices of the Methodist Episcopal Church in the United States of America, an institution for the promotion of education and investigation in science, literature, and art, do hereby certify as follows:

*First,* The name of said institution is "The American University."

*Second,* The number of the trustees thereof is twenty; [their names]; the said trustees may enlarge their number to fifty and fill all vacancies therein; at all times at least two-thirds of the Trustees and also the Chancellor of the said university shall be members of the aforesaid Methodist Episcopal Church, and all trustees elected after the 1st day of December, A. D. 1891, shall be submitted to the General Conference of said Church for its approval.

*Third,* All branches of science, literature, and art (and more especially the highest departments in each) are to be taught in said university.

*Fourth,* The number and designation of the professorships to be established in said university is to be sufficient to successfully equip, direct, and develop each department of instruction therein.

The trustees of this university have secured a handsome and commanding site, in a desirable suburban district, at an expense of $100,000, generously furnished by citizens of Washington, have started a monthly publication for the advocacy of the enterprise in the country, and are actively engaged in raising contributions to the proposed endowment of $10,000,000, with the declared purpose, however, not to begin operations until the sum of $5,000,000 shall have been secured.

It should be added that the enterprise was formally indorsed by the General Conference at its last session, on which occasion many speeches were made in its support. By way of illustrating the spirit of the movement brief extracts are made from a number of the addresses on that occasion.[1]

From the address of Bishop Newman:

Great thoughts never die. The American University had its genesis in George Washington. His great compatriot, Hamilton, scholar, statesman, and orator, young and brilliant, drafted a comprehensive plan of national education, with its controlling

[1] The American University and the General Conference, May, 1892.

institution in the city of Washington; at once the source of authority and the power of direction for all institutions of learning, from the primary department to a well-equipped university for original investigation and for professional study. Both Washington and Hamilton conceived the idea that the highest intelligence is indispensable to the welfare and perpetuity of the Republic; and believing in this, they sought to lay plans for the consummation of such a desirable end, an end to be sanctified by virtue born of Chistianity. But the proposition excited contention. The cry of centralization vexed the very skies of the Republic, and the jealousy incident to the rule of State rights compelled Washington and Hamilton to delay the consummation of their wise and beneficent purpose.   *   *   *

In view of these sad effects there are three things we should demand: First, a national system of education under the General Government, with its head a Cabinet officer; second, a system of compulsory education in every State and Territory; and, third, no appropriation by the nation, or by any State, or municipality for any sectarian institution in any part of the land.

As I said, great thoughts never die. So it is true in regard to this. A hundred years have passed, but during that century the thought of an American university has been conspicuous in the teachings of the great jurists and statesmen of the past and has been the dominant thought of those master minds, Jay and Kent and Marshall, and in our days of the scholarly Sumner and that great jurist of Vermont, Edmunds.

*          *          *          *          *          *          *

Providence ordains the times and seasons according to an infinite wisdom, and raises up men to accomplish the exalted purposes of Jehovah. Educated carefully at home and abroad, gifted with an imagination that frescos the future with the actualities of the present, endowed with the rare power of organization to prepare great plans for the oncoming generations, it comes to us more and more that in the roll of the centuries, in the ordering of time, God Almighty, the God of our fathers, has selected Bishop Hurst to lay the foundation of the American University for American Methodism.

### From the address of Rev. Dr. Payne:

The time has come for a fuller recognition of the fact that the character of the work now to be done by the Church demands the highest qualities in the workmen employed. Methodism proposes to do her full share in taking this world for Christ in the shortest possible time; and her full share is a large share. To meet her responsibilities and fulfill her mission she must have the best officers and best commanded army in Christendom.   *   *   *

And to secure the best educational institutions makes necessary the best educational system, the wisest connectional care and supervision, and a loyal, united, enthusiastic rallying of this vast Methodistic host to the support of its own educational institutions and work.   *   *   *

Methodism is building for a vast future and for uncounted millions. Let us build this glorious temple of Methodism with its marble front toward the future; build for the coming generations, build for all the years of time and eternity.

### From the address of Bishop Fowler:

In this war of the giants our champions must not be wanting. This American University, located at the heart of the nation, not far from the most distant home, with vast accumulations of appliances, and to offer the utmost possible advantages, can not wait long for any good thing. We can not afford to miss our opportunity. God never forgives a blunder. History moves forward, and destiny approaches by the most certain and discernible laws. Spain can not consign scores of thousands of her most industrious, most intelligent subjects to the torture of the Inquisition without suffering severe loss in her wealth. It is not the most profitable use to make of able and skilled citizens. No wonder Spain was transferred from the banker to the pauper of the race.   *   *   *

These blunders are never forgiven. If we fail to see our day of opportunity, we shall drop into the rear, and cease to do our part for the evangelization of this land and this world, and that sad voice from the broken-hearted watcher of Olivet will come to us: "O Methodism, Methodism; if thou hadst known, even thou, at least in this thy day, the things which belong to thy peace!"

### From the address of Rev. Dr. McCabe:

If the past is prophetic of the future, this American University will have much to do with the cause of missions. The name of a university professor is a household word in Methodism, because it is connected with that all-conquering theology which is believeable and preachable, and which is destined to take the world—James Arminius, of the University of Leyden. * * *

Now it is our purpose to establish in Washington a training school for missionries, where they will have every facility to learn languages and customs and manners of the countries to which we propose to send them. * * *

Another feature of our work will be to bring to our country the highest minds of the Orient and educate them, and send them back to their homes saturated with the love of liberty and the love of God and of His Son Jesus Christ.

### From the address of Rev. Dr. Bashford:

The cost of maintaining the *college* in a large city, the diversion of young and immature minds through the entertainments of city life, the prevalence of the commercial spirit, and, above all, the difficulty of bringing spiritual forces to bear in the most effective manner, may lead the Church for generations to maintain her colleges in more retired localities. But the great cities are absolutely essential to university work. The demand for concentration and study amidst the whirl of business and entertainment is in itself a discipline for professional students. The great hospitals and courts of law, the leading pulpits, the galleries of art, and the great libraries are absolutely essential to the professional student. But what great city is more favorable to university work than the capital of the nation? The University of Paris at the capital of France, is the largest university in the world. The history of the University of Berlin is a more striking illustration of this principle. It is a modern university, organized less than a century ago. It was planted in a nation full of universities. And yet with the marvelous advantages of the capital of that great empire Berlin University has become within three-quarters of a century the leading university of the world.

### From the address of Bishop Thoburn:

Every nation, like every individual, has a personal mission, a personal responsibility. God gives to a nation as to an individual an opportunity. He lays upon every nation its responsibility. A nation will be held responsible for what is given it, as an individual would be. The position of America is unique. There has never been a great power in human history that occupied such a position as we occupy in the world to-day; and I think one of the great questions which the American people have not yet fully settled is that of the mission of their own nation in the world. I fear the prevailing opinion is that we have been put in this western world, with superb opportunities, simply that we might become the greatest people on the globe. If that foolish conceit takes possession of us, as a people, we are lost. * * * My own conviction has long been that the mission of America in the world is that of being the missionary nation of modern times—a great agent in the hands of God in bringing all the nations of this world to Christ. * * *

Education maintains a prominent place in mission work, and I believe that in the fullness of time this university idea has been started.

### From the address of Rev. Dr. Moore:

But the university period has only dawned in America. Its harbingers have been many, but itself is not older than the opening of Johns Hopkins. It must certainly be gratifying to Methodists that thus early the plans are matured and the enterprise auspiciously inaugurated to found in our national capital a Methodist institution, which shall be an university in the broadest sense of the term, the scope of whose work is suggested by the fact that it does not propose to open its doors until it has an endowment greater than that gathered by all the institutions of our church in a hundred years.

---

CIV. The action of the Human Freedom League at the time of its organization in Independence Hall, Philadelphia, on the 11th of October, 1891, by resolution including among its duties and responsibilities that of promoting the establishment of a national university; said resolution being as follows:

(3) To take up the work outlined by George Washington in his will, whereby he left a large share of his property for the purpose of endowing a university where the youth of the country might be educated in statecraft, and push the same to a successful conclusion. Such a university should be national, and yet have its doors always open to the youth of every land.

CV. The reading of a paper entitled, "The National Debt of Honor," by Dr. George Brown Goode, of the Smithsonian Institution, at a meeting of the general committee of the Pan-Republic Congress, held in the Academy of Music at Philadelphia, on the 13th of October, 1891; which paper, besides presenting the main facts of Washington's efforts for a national university, as herein mentioned, strongly urges the obligation of the nation, not only to establish and liberally endow such an institution, but to make good the full amount of the bequest intended by him to be the beginning of its endowment, and concludes with an indorsement of the national committee's plan of the proposed institution, and with a moving appeal in behalf of the great enterprise:

Congress has, however, failed to extend its direct patronage to any educational enterprise of the highest grade. Unlike most of the governments of the old world, it supports no faculties of learned men whose duty it is to discover truth and give it to the world. It has not yet provided a national university so excellent that it is not necessary, in the language of Washington, "for the youth of the United States to migrate to foreign countries in order to acquire the higher branches of education." While it has established a great system of schools under the patronage of the several States, it has failed to provide a central institution which shall serve as a model for all the others, train teachers for their faculties, afford their scholars post-graduate instruction, and add character and dignity, intellectual and moral, to the nation's capital. * * *

The sum of $4,401,000 [amount of Washington's bequest with compound interest to the present time], if appropriated for this purpose by Congress, and placed in the Treasury of the United States, there to remain paying interest at 6 per cent, would yield over $264,000 each year, a sum that would provide for many professorships, lectureships and scholarships, and fellowships, as well as for the current expenses of several seminaries or colleges. Private gifts would in time be added in large amounts, and Congress would of course erect such buildings as from time to time were found necessary. * * *

Among the various plans for the organization and government of a national university, that proposed by Governor John W, Hoyt, of Wyoming, and embodied in a bill unanimously reported by a committee of the House of Representatives, in 1873, is by far the best, and, in its practical features, seems all that could be desired. This bill received the approval of Charles Sumner, Joseph Henry, Louis Agassiz, Spencer F. Baird, John Eaton, William T. Harris, as well as many other distinguished citizens, and had the sanction of the National Educational Association.

CVI. The adoption, by the Pan-Republic ·Congress General Committee of Three Hundred, of the following preamble and resolution offered by John W. Hoyt, at the conclusion of the paper read by Dr. Goode, of the Smithsonian Institution, on the 13th of October, 1891, as above recited:

Whereas, this general committee, formed for the purpose of advancing the cause of peace and liberal government throughout the world by means of a succession of congresses of the representatives of all civilized lands, could yet further contribute to these great ends by encouraging such organizations and enterprises as look to the increase of knowledge and of liberal thought among men; and

Whereas, it is manifest that a truly national university established at the seat of government of the United States, and aiming, first, to crown the present incomplete system of American education; secondly, to promote the advancement of knowledge by means of the researches and investigations of its members as well as by its influence upon the science and learning of other lands; and, finally, to encourage a larger intellectual intercourse and community of feeling among the leading minds of the world, would at once prove conservative of our own free institutions, strengthen the bonds of fraternity among all peoples, and contribute to the betterment of governmental institutions everywhere; and

Whereas, it appears from the records of history, not only that on this very spot sacred to liberty and independence the importance of such a university was urged by the framers of the American Constitution, but that several of the Presidents, including George Washington, John Adams, Thomas Jefferson, James Madison, James Monroe, John Quincy Adams, Ulysses S. Grant, and Rutherford B. Hayes, pressed its early establishment as a patriotic duty; that President Washington even remembered it with a liberal gift in his dying bequest; * * that the proposition to establish it has been sanctioned by other leading statesmen throughout the period of our national history, and, finally, that such proposition has been thrice unanimously indorsed by that great body of American educators, the National Educational Association; therefore,

Resolved, That in order to aid in the founding of such an institution, the chairman of this general committee is hereby requested to appoint a special committee consisting of one or more members from each of the States and Territories, whose duty it shall to be adopt and carry forward such measures to this end as to them shall seem proper; reporting to this committee in their discretion, or as required from time to time, and in particular at the time and place of the Pan-Republic Congress to be held in the year 1893.

The following committee was appointed:

John W. Hoyt, Laramie, Wyo., chairman; Dr. G. Browne Goode, Smithsonian Institution; ex-President Andrew D. White, Ithaca, N. Y.; Dr. Edward Everett Hale, Boston; President A. S. Andrews, Southern University, Greensboro, Ala.; Rev. Dr. Geo. D. Boardman, Philadelphia; Dr. Chas. B. Cadwallader, Philadelphia; President Thomas J. Burrell, University of Illinois; Hon. J. W. Anderson, State superintendent public instruction, Sacramento, Cal.; Hon. Harvey L. Vories, State superintendent public instruction, Indianapolis, Ind.; President John R. Winston, University of North Carolina, Chapel Hill; Dr. James Hall, State geologist, Albany, N. Y.; ex-President Horace M. Hale,

University of Colorado; Hon. Edwin F. Palmer, State superintendent public instruction, Waterbury, Vt.; ex-Senator J. W. Patterson, Concord, N. H.; Dr. James Grant Wilson, New York City; Hon. Albert J. Russell, State superintendent public instruction, Tallahassee, Fla.; Hon. Cortez Salmon, State superintendent public instruction, Pierre, S. Dak.; President Francis E. Nipher, Academy of Science, St. Louis, Mo.; Dr. Charles C. Jones, Augusta, Ga.; Hon. J. R. Preston, State superintendent public instruction, Jackson, Miss.; Dr. M. Schele de Vere, University of Virginia; Hon. William Wirt Henry, Richmond, Va.; President Newton Bateman, Knox College, Galesburg, Ill.; Hon. J. W. Dickinson, secretary State board of education, Boston, Mass.; Hon. Thomas B. Stockwell, State commissioner of schools, Providence, R. I.; Dr. Frank H. Kasson, editor of Education, Boston, Mass.; Dr. H. B. Adams, Johns Hopkins University, Baltimore, Md.; President T. C. Chamberlin, State University of Wisconsin, Madison, Wis.; Rt. Rev. Ethelbert Talbot, Protestant Episcopal bishop of Wyoming and Idaho; Hon. S. M. Finger, State superintendent public instruction, Raleigh, N. C.; President J. C. Gilchrist, University of Northwest, Pierre, S. Dak.; Hon. Gardner G. Hubbard, Washington, D. C.; Col. W. O. McDowell, editor of *Home and Country*, Newark, N. J.

CVII. The address of John W. Hoyt before the Philosophical Society, at Washington, in October, 1891, by request of that body.

CVIII. The preparation and wide circulation, by John W. Hoyt, of a leaflet late in 1891, wherein were set forth the claims of the proposed National University; the same being an outline of this present paper, to wit:

A great and true university the leading want of American education.
The offices of a true university.
Reasons why the Government should establish such a university.
Reasons for founding such a university at Washington.
Summary of the notable efforts hitherto made in this behalf.
Reasons for a renewal of such efforts at this time.
The proposition of to-day.
The conditions of success.

CIX. The interest manifested in various ways and at different times during the past twenty years by numerous distinguished citizens in all portions of the country, including, besides those already named:
(1) Such leading educators as—

President Thomas Hill, of Cambridge, Mass.; President F. A. P. Barnard, of Columbia College, New York; President Alexander W. Winchell, of Syracuse University, New York; President Erastus O. Haven, of Michigan University; President J. L. Pickard, of Iowa State University; President Paul A. Chadbourne, of Wisconsin State University; Dr. Henry Barnard, United States Commissioner of Education; President J. M. Gregory, of Illinois State University; President J. M. Bowman, of Kentucky University; President W. G. Elliot, of Washington University, St. Louis; President Newton Bateman, of Knox College, Illinois; President David S. Jordan, of Leland Stanford, jr., University; President George T. Winston, University of Mississippi; Dr. M. Schele de Vere, University of Virginia; President A. S. Andrews, of the Southern University, Alabama; President Thomas J. Burrill, University of Illinois; President T. C. Chamberlin, University of Wisconsin; President Horace M. Hale, University of Colorado; President James B. Angell, University of Michigan; President Francis Wayland, of Brown University.

(2) Superintendents of public instruction in nearly all the States; the unanimity and cordiality of their support resulting from a conviction of the great service a national university would render to the whole system of public schools.

(3) Such eminent scholars, scientists, and promoters of science as—

Rt. Rev. Bishop Alonzo Potter, New York; Dr. Henry P. Tappan, chancellor of the University of Michigan; Prof. Arnold Henry Guyot, Princeton; Dr. Alex. Dallas Bache, early superintendent of Coast Survey; Prof. Benjamin Peirce, former superintendent of Coast Survey; Prof. Spencer F. Baird, former Secretary of Smithsonian Institution; Prof. H. V. Hayden, United States Geologist; Prof. John W. Powell, Director of the U. S. Geological Survey; Prof. Benjamin Apthorp Gould, astronomer; Prof. Ormsby M. Mitchell, astronomer; Prof. J. Lawrence Smith, president American Association Advancement of Science; Admiral Sands, former Superintendent of National Observatory; Lieut. M. F. Maury, former Superintendent of the Naval Observatory; Dr. S. P. Langley, present Secretary of the Smithsonian Institution; Dr. Simon Newcomb, Superintendent of the Nautical Almanac; Prof. James C. Watson, astronomer, Michigan and Wisconsin State Universities; Prof. T. C. Mendenhall, present Superintendent of the Coast Survey; Dr. James Hall, State geologist, New York; Dr. F. Nipher, president Academy of Science, St. Louis; Hon. Edwin Willits, Assistant Secretary of Agriculture; Dr. Mark W. Harrington, Chief of the Weather Bureau; Dr. J. S. Billings, Superintendent United States Medical Museum; Gen. A. W. Greely, Chief of the United States Signal Office; Gardner G. Hubbard, president National Geographical Society; Dr. Persifer Frazer, of Philadelphia; Rt. Rev. William Paret, Bishop of Maryland; Rt. Rev. Thomas M. Clark, of Providence; President William R. Harper, University of Chicago; Prof. Hinsdale, of Michigan University; Dr. J. C. Pumpelly, of New York; Dr. Clark Ridpath, of Indiana; Prof. E. P. Powell, of New York; Dr. Edward Everett Hale, of Massachusetts; Dr. Frank W. Kassou, editor of Education; Dr. James Grant Wilson, of New York; Rt. Rev. Thos. A. Starkey, Bishop of Newark.

(4) Such distinguished statesmen, not already cited, as—

Ex-President Grover Cleveland, Chief Justice Salmon P. Chase, Gen. W. T. Sherman, Senator Justin S. Morrill, Senator Carl Schurz, Senator Stanley Matthews, Senator James R. Doolittle, Senator Redfield Proctor, Senator John Sherman, Senator Charles F. Manderson, Senator W. F. Vilas; also, many members of the House of Representatives, such as Samuel Shellabarger, George F. Hoar, James A. Garfield, and William A. Wilson.

CX. The steps already taken toward the organization of a National University Association of the United States, to be composed of many of the most eminent citizens of the country, and to have for its sole object the furtherance of this great enterprise.

———

In view of this record of more than a hundred years, showing how deeply the subject of a National University has interested a great number of citizens, not a few of them foremost in the history of the Republic, the question arises, Why all this effort with so little of visible result?

The answer is not difficult. At the opening of this paper certain positive hindrances were pointed out and commented upon. Although these have been almost entirely overcome in the natural course of events, so that to-day they do not appear an important factor, yet it is true that throughout the greater part of the period since the movement was begun by George Washington they were together sufficient to cause much embarrassment and long delay. But there is also to be assigned a negative reason of very great importance, namely, the lack of systematic coöperation on the part of those who have been friends of the measure.

Steps in this direction were taken in the palmy days of Joseph Henry, Alexander Dallas Bache, Louis Agassiz, James Apthorp Gould, James Hall, Bishop Potter of New York, Prof. Benjamin Peirce, and their many distinguished associates, as we have seen, but were not persevered in because of the gathering of the storm which shortly after burst with so much fury upon the country. The same is also partly true of the university committee of the National Educational Association, whose labors were interrupted for a time by the circumstances hereinbefore mentioned, but whose active work has been at length resumed with even more than the old zeal and energy.

It is certainly true, in a general sense, that the National University cause has been without the necessary help of organized agencies. The great amount of work done has been individual, intermittent, unrelated; and hence it is that all who are in sympathy with the enterprise may hail with satisfaction, as the concluding memorandum of this summary, the announcement of such coöperation of forces in future as will prove helpful to the worthy statesmen destined to be effective leaders of the movement in Congress, and thus assure to it an earlier victory.

# V.

## REASONS FOR RENEWED EFFORT AT THIS TIME.

The chief reasons for reviving the question at this time are these:

First. The general education bill, so long before Congress, having been disposed of, there is no longer any obligation on the part of the friends of the national university proposition to remain quiescent, as they were willing to do while they who were committed to that measure were still hopeful of victory.

Second. The failure of the general education bill should but constitute a new reason for the passage of a bill to establish a great university. Not alone because, having failed to pass one measure in the interest of education, Congress should be all the more ready, and find it the more easy, to favor another of equal or greater importance, but also because the chief objection to that measure in no manner applies to this one. For, if it be true that the people in the several States, districts, and neighborhoods are abundantly able to provide schools of the lower grade for the youth of the land, the same is certainly not true of the people in their local and individual capacity in relation to a central university of the highest type. No one man, no one community, no one State is equal to the establishment of such an institution. And if that were possible, in so far as means are concerned, still it is manifest that neither community nor State, nor even the most powerful of the religious organizations, could possibly establish and maintain a national university. That is a sole prerogative of the whole people in their legislative capacity. On Congress alone that great obligation rests.

Third. The present condition of the country, now fairly recovered from the industrial and commercial depression of recent years, with new buoyancy of spirit, and with hopes well founded on census returns that astonish the world and establish our superiority among the nations, is exceedingly favorable. It is now beyond question that the Government of the United States could henceforth pay at least a million a year as interest on a registered certificate and not feel the draft in any degree.

Fourth. It is no less true that the public mind, which in recent years has been slowly but surely coming to the opinion that President Hill, of Harvard, was right when in his last official report he said "a true university is a leading want of American education," is now ready to undertake the supply of that want.

As we have seen, prominent educators, leading scholars, and scientists, distinguished statesmen, and great organizations of men, educa-

114

tional, scientific, literary, patriotic, and philanthropic, have strongly confirmed the truth of this declaration; while powerful organizations of the church, both Catholic and Protestant, have also considered the question, resolved, and begun to act. It is seen that the rapid growth and present enormous value of university facilities at Washington are now so well known as to constitute a great attraction for students, scholars, and scientists the world over when brought into relations with a national university.

Fifth. This circumstance of a movement for a university at Washington, by two powerful church organizations is highly favorable to the early establishment of a national university. They are both of them effective agitators of great questions, and will be preëminently influential with the masses, who alone of all the people may need to be convinced. Both because of their philanthropic aims and of the helpful pioneer work they will of necessity do, we may bid such organized efforts Godspeed. There is room enough for all. Should they each succeed in founding an important institution they will simply swell the grand chorus and contribute yet more to make of the national capital the intellectual center of the world.

And if, on the other hand, seeing that the nation itself is to found the American university, they and the multitude of like organizations should each see fit to concentrate their efforts upon great schools of theology to be clustered about the national university as a high central source of general instruction and of inspiration for all, then this grand unity of all in the cause of pure learning and of progress in science and the arts would only yet more enhance the dignity of the university itself, yet further promote the great interests of American education, and contribute yet more to brighten the halo which already encircles the brow of the Republic.

Sixth. The present is also a favorable time from a political point of view, since with the present constitution of the national legislature the honor of founding the proposed institution may and must be equally shared by the two great political parties; since, moreover, there is reason to believe that of late there have been important accessions in both Houses of Congress to the very considerable body of members known to have been favorable to this enterprise from the beginning of its agitation in recent years.

Seventh. The present time is auspicious for the reason that numbers of men of vast fortunes and of honorable ambitions are now in the spirit of making large contributions to education. The Hopkinses, Vanderbilts, Drexels, Clarks, Tulanes, Rockefellers, Stanfords, Carnegies, and Fayrweathers have only set examples which a much larger number are preparing to follow. And hence it is again urged that if Congress should now establish and liberally endow the national university, gifts of many millions for the founding of fellowships, professorships, faculties, and departments, would flow into its treasury as contributions to the vast aggregate sum that will thus constitute its final endowment.

Eighth. Now is the appointed time for historic reasons. Action by the present Congress would enable us to make the beginnings of the national university a part of the great Columbian celebration in 1893, and its proper inauguration a most fitting centennial commemoration of Washington's last earnest appeal in its behalf to the people and Congress of the United States, in 1796. It was with the help of science that Christopher Columbus found these wonderful new continents, and hence America could not more truly honor him than by inaugurating on the four hundredth anniversary of his discovery an institution of learning sublimely dedicated not alone to the diffusion of knowledge, but also to the discovery of unnumbered continents of truth in the coming centuries. The Columbian Exposition will of itself be a grand but a vanishing monument. Let us also, in commemoration of the achievements of 1492, found here an institution that shall lead the world in its grand career of progress, and proudly endure through all future time.

And what of Washington, with all his eloquent pleadings and his dying bequest, added to achievements in behalf of his country and of universal freedom which have made him immortal? The Centennial Exposition of 1876 was a worthy commemoration of those heroic beginnings which led to American independence and the founding of a great nation, but it was for the honoring of all alike who had part in the grand drama of the Revolution. Do not the hearts of the American people prompt to some centennial recognition of the supreme services and example of him whom the world delights to call the Father of His Country? True, on that beautiful swell of ground near the Potomac he loved stands a proud shaft of marble whose whiteness symbolizes his purity and whose towering summit suggests that stateliness and that loftiness of character for which he was so incomparable that he has seemed to be unapproachable—a shaft that plainly shows the place he holds in the affections of the people, and which also honors the multitudes out of whose contributions it was erected.

But is that enough? There was One who said, "If a man ask bread, will ye give him a stone?" And yet is not this what we have literally done? Twelve times in formal utterance, and times untold in familiar speech and silent prayer, he who had rescued his country from the grasp of tyranny and laid for it the deep foundations on which this great Republic was reared asked for a university that should supply to this people the bread of knowledge, and we have builded for him a monument of stone! Shall we not at last redeem ourselves from his just reproach and the reproach of succeeding generations by such granting of his request as shall fittingly atone for the neglect of a hundred years?

Finally, there is a reason broader and more far-reaching than all of these, one in which a genuine patriotism mingles with a pure philanthropy in equal measure. During the past several years the American people have celebrated many great and stirring events in American history.

It is well. Such celebrations serve at once to keep in remembrance the heroic deeds of a noble ancestry, and to deepen in the hearts of the people their love of country and their appreciation of free institutions; but they will have failed of their highest use after all if they do not arouse in us a like zeal in the interest of country and human kind. We need not wait for occasions precisely theirs. The opportunity is ever present. It is not by glorying in the deeds of our sires, but by great and honorable deeds of our own that we are to stand approved. We must continue to rear upon the foundations they laid such superstructures as will make at once for the further prosperity and security of our country and for the peace and progress of the world. Having fitly celebrated the past, shall we not now face about and begin anew the great work of the coming century? Was it not in this spirit that were formed the many patriotic organizations we now see on every hand, with their efforts not alone for general progress but also for the perfect cementing of all sections of the American Union and for peace and concord among the nations? And what better beginning on the intellectual side of so beneficent and glorious a mission than the founding of a great university, comprehensive not only of all present knowledge, with competent agencies for its diffusion among men, but also of wisely directed efforts for the discovery of new truth as well as for new applications of knowledge in the common interest of mankind—an institution so supreme, *toto cœlo*, so consecrated to the highest good of humanity, and so truly a guiding star in the intellectual firmament as to be gladly recognized and accepted of all the nations of the world?

# VI.

## THE DEMAND OF THE PRESENT.

What the friends of education now ask is this: That the Government of the United States, after more than a hundred years since the earnest appeals and final bequest of Washington, at length extend the needed "fostering hand" to that great enterprise of which he fondly believed he had made a worthy beginning; that Congress now begin the establishment of a true national university in harmony with the general principles already set forth by what may be regarded as the highest authorities on this subject—

A university, whose board of regents, representing all sections, shall be so chosen and so limited when chosen as not only to insure the promotion of its general interests, but also to avoid the dangers of partisan interference, religious or political;

Whose provision for internal management shall duly protect the interests of learning and the rights of all members;

Whose conditions of admission shall relate to character and competency only;

The doors of whose regular courses of study, looking to graduation, shall be open to such only as have already received the bachelor's degree from recognized institutions;

Whose students of every class shall be permitted to utilize the vast facilities and forces in the many Departments of the Government so far as this can be accorded without detriment to the public service;

Whose system of scholarships shall supply at once a reward of merit and a stimulus to the youth of the country in every grade of schools, shall hold the schools themselves to proper standards, and insure the highest character of the university membership;

Whose fellowships shall be open to all the nations and so endowed as to fill its places for original work with aspirants of superior genius from every quarter of the globe;

Whose professoriate, like that of the German universities, shall by its system of gradations and promotions supply its professorships and lectureships with the best talent and proficiency the world can afford;

Whose graduates, receiving none but the higher degrees, shall be to all the schools, colleges, and universities of the land a means of reënforcement from the highest possible source;

Whose high faculties of letters, science, and philosophy shall be the center of a grand constellation of ranking schools for all the professions save theology, with surrounding of such independent religious institutions as the hundreds of denominations may choose to set up;

Whose beginnings shall be with such means as befit the great undertaking, and whose final aggregation of endowments by Government, States, organizations, and philanthropists, shall fully comport with the demands of learning, with the aspirations of a great people of surpassing genius as well as material resources, and with the incalculable interest of other peoples in those free institutions which, being ours by inheritance, it is our solemn duty to perfect and illustrate for the best good of universal man.

According to the plan of endowment once proposed—that of issuing a registered certificate unassignable and bearing interest at a fixed rate in perpetuity—there need be no considerable draft upon the present money resources of the Government. It is now paying out more than three millions for the support and development of its invaluable scientific bureaus, libraries, and museums. Let it now add a million more to this sum for the support of an institution equal to the task of further, and as completely as possible, utilizing the vast collections and forces already here, and it will render an incalcuable service to the cause of learning, the country, and the world.

As it was the university of Paris that brought new prosperity and distinction to France, and the university of Berlin that helped immensely to build up the little Kingdom of Prussia into the majestic Empire of Germany, thus creating two intellectual centers whose achievements are the envy of the world, so will the National University of America, if thus established and endowed, powerfully contribute to place the United States in the forefront of the nations.

# VII.

## THE CONDITIONS OF SUCCESS.

First, they who are in power must give the matter its full measure of consideration. Absorbed in other matters, pressed by measures of finance, commerce, lands, industrial development, and much else, even the most intelligent and large-minded of men are in danger of over-looking a measure, however important, comprehensive, and far-reaching, that is neither vital to party success nor boldly insists on being heard.

Secondly, while it may be assumed that such of our statesmen as already appreciate the importance of the enterprise, seeing clearly how it would promote the national welfare and advance the cause of learning in the world, are equal to the responsibility of taking it up and carrying it forward to a successful issue on the high ground of duty alone, it is but right as well as desirable that they be duly reënforced by the enlightened sentiment of the country. And they certainly will be. Educators at the head of our schools, academies, colleges, and universities, with the multitude of their friends, none of whom can fail to see the incalculable value of a crowning institution like the one proposed, will naturally join hands for its early realization when they discover an earnest purpose in Congress.

Last, but not least, the press of the United States, so liberal and ever on the alert for new measures of progress, can be safely counted on to more fully interest the general public in a proposition so often urged by the Father of his Country, so repeatedly indorsed by other of our statesmen in all periods of the national history, and so clearly a condition of the highest dignity and welfare of the Republic.

Such opposition as may manifest itself in any form will disappear on a nearer, more scrutinizing, and broader view.

The old and once popular objection to government institutions on the ground of "political" interference, has long ceased to be valid as against Congressionally-endowed State institutions, many of which are now among the most important in the land, and is sufficiently met by the adoption of such provisions as are embodied in charters wisely drawn in the sole interest of learning—charters under which there is seldom occasion for submitting to the legislature such questions as could be made to assume a partisan form, which leave the internal affairs of such an institution almost entirely in the hands of its professional members, themselves governed by university laws which give both security and efficiency to the entire service.

120

No institutions in the land are better managed or have larger immunity from partisan interference than our State universities, and none are more prosperous. Indeed one of these, the University of Michigan, is in point of numbers the strongest institution in America, having in all its numerous departments nearly three thousand students. And not only in point of numbers does it hold high ground. For the character of its many departments, the number and ability of its professors, its standard of scholarship, and skill of general management, it stands in the front rank. Peace reigns within its borders, the whole people regard it with pride, and the legislature accords to it a cheerful and generous support. In one respect, that of exerting a guiding and elevating influence upon all the lower schools of the State, in a manner similar to that proposed for the national university, it has long been foremost; affording a most useful example to all other State universities.

The extraordinary career of the Smithsonian Institution, always free from even the slightest taint of " politics," and already become the most important institution of its kind in the world, affords yet another total refutation of this ancient theory that no interest, of however exalted a nature, may come to be sacred in the eyes of political ambition.

In fact, with the growing respect for science and learning, and the consequent spirit of an honorable rivalry among the higher institutions of the country, especially those of them annually reporting to the Government, there has come an almost total emancipation from the once potent influence of political partisanship. The supreme interest involved has so far determined both legislative and executive action in the several States that scrupulous care is coming to be taken everywhere to balance the control of all such public institutions so evenly as to leave no room for the jealous scheming of parties.

Time has also settled another question. The old argument against a national university, based on the centralization theory, has long perished from the earth. It was early shown to be unphilosophical, and time has added countless illustrations of its falsity. The error was in making no radical distinction between a centralization of political power, which always demands vigilance lest it advance to the point of endangering the liberties of the people, and centralization of educational opportunities, which is not only absolutely necessary to the highest results in the interest of learning, but is itself the best safeguard against the encroachments of political ambition by furnishing to thousands of local centers trained thinkers who are also, in the very process of training, imbued with the spirit of liberty and independence. Every intelligent citizen now knows that, while political centralization is like a congestion, fatal if carried to a certain limit, educational centralization is, on the other hand, like the concentration of the vital fluid in the heart—a prerequisite to that diffusion of knowledge which insures health and security to every part of the body politic.

Opposition based on local ambitions will also disappear when a just view is taken of the relation that is normally sustained by a central and national post-graduate university to all other institutions; when it is once seen how potential for the good of all would be that central co-ordinating and uplifting force to which allusion has been made; how powerfully the national university would inspire every faculty of instruction and every ambitious institution of learning in the land; how, with open doors for those worthy to enter them, it would in turn prove a great training school for such as might desire chairs in the nearly five hundred colleges and universities of the country; how by its exalted service and by the supreme dignity through it and for its sake accorded to science and learning it would reflect new honor upon all institutions of learning wheresoever found.

It is a source of high gratification that this view is already shared by the great body of educators in the United States, as must have appeared from the foregoing summary, and especially gratifying that almost without exception the presidents of great and growing universities, North, South, East, and West, have warmly declared their sympathy with the national university movement.

There has not been named in all the past, nor can there be named in any future, one argument against the national university proposition of George Washington that will bear the scrutiny of philosophy or the test of history.

# VIII.

## CONCLUSION.

This present labor may now be concluded. It has been shown—

That the offices of a true university, although of the most important character, are not all of them now duly fulfilled in this country;

That these offices could be best fulfilled by a great national university, and that such university would be most conveniently, suitably, and advantageously established and maintained at the seat of the National Government; where the chief elements of a university exist already, needing but their organization, suitable halls for instructional purposes, and means for the support of a large and superior working force;

That certain functions, vital in their character, that would be performed by a national institution, to wit, the completement of an American system of public education, the coördination and highest development of the schools of the States, and the most effectual cultivation of the patriotic sentiment in the minds of those certain to be potential in the direction of our national affairs, *can be performed by none other than a truly National University;*

That this conception, originating in the mind of General Washington during the stormy days of the Revolution, and cherished by him through life with a fondness and constancy only matched by his love of country, has also engaged the thoughts of many other statesmen, as well of leading citizens in every walk of life; that Congressional committees have favorably considered it, and that national organizations founded in the interest of learning and of human progress have made earnest appeals for its realization;

That the need of a central American university, thus recognized and thus urged, not only remains, notwithstanding the development of existing institutions, but for important national reasons increases with the years;

That such institution could be established and endowed without heavy drafts upon the National Treasury; and

That this present is in all respects a favorable time for the final fulfillment of a solemn duty so long delayed.

It can not be doubted that a nation of such vast resources in every realm, of such superior intelligence, and of such aspirations and aims, has already come to realize what is due in this high regard; due to its own members craving the opportunities such a university would offer, due to the sacred cause of learning, due to the honor and welfare of a Republic rightfully ambitious to lead all the nations in the grand march of civilization.

○

•

# OF THE NATIONAL UNIVERSITY PRO-
# POSED BY GEORGE WASHINGTON.

PREPARED BY EX-GOV. JOHN W. HOYT, LL.D.

*Chairman of National University Committees.*

[Taken, by permission, from the advance sheets of THE ARENA for March.]

GREAT, indeed, were the wisdom, patriotism, generalship, and statesmanship of the immortal Washington. Hardly less remarkable, in view of the conditions of his life, were his estimates of the priceless value of learning as a means of promoting the security and general welfare of the new American republic; the profound interest he manifested in adequate provision for the intellectual culture of the whole people ; the prescience with which he anticipated the demand for a crowning central institution to be established and fostered by the Federal Government; the deep solicitude and self-sacrificing devotion with which, even from the midst of the Revolutionary War to the end of life, he persisted in efforts for a national university.

Surprising, also, is the fact, so full of reproach for succeeding generations, that this great idea of Washington, so steadily . fostered for a quarter of a century, has not even yet been realized. Is it not fitting, then, that on the day set apart as sacred to his memory, we revive the recollection of —

His many efforts even before the actual founding of the Government.

His inaugural address, January 8, 1790.

His letter of November 27, 1794, to John Adams, Vice-President.

His letter of December 15, 1794, to Mr. Randolph, Secretary of State.

His letter to the Commissioners of the District of Columbia.

His letter to Thomas Jefferson, March 15, 1795.

His letter to Governor Brooke, of Virginia, March 16, 1795.

His two letters to Alexander Hamilton, September 1 and September 6, 1796.

His letter to the Commissioners of the District of Columbia, designating a site.

His last message to Congress.

His dying bequest, leaving as a beginning of a pecuniary foundation a sum which, had it been cared for by the Government, in accordance with the stipulations of his last will and testament, would by this time have amounted to nearly five millions of dollars.

No wonder that one hears on all sides the questions, "Why this great neglect?" "Have there been no other champions of a cause so important, and now become sacred?"

Aye, champions indeed! Illustrious champions, and in great numbers, as you shall see.

Deeply sharing Washington's patriotic aspirations, James Madison, Charles C. Pickering, Benjamin Franklin, William Samuel Johnson, and other distinguished members of the Constitutional Convention of 1787 sought to incorporate a provision for the proposed National University in the Constitution itself, and only yielded to the general judgment that the exclusive authority of Congress over the District of Columbia, already provided for, obviated the necessity for any specific provision, and to the desire of all that nothing superfluous should have place in that great instrument.

There, too, was Dr. Benjamin Rush, signer of the Declaration of Independence, and leading scientist of his time, who in the very year of the Convention made eloquent pleas such as this :

Your Government cannot be executed ; it is too expensive for a republic ; it is contrary to the habits of the people, say the enemies of the Constitution of the United States. However opposite to the opinions and wishes of a majority of the citizens of the United States these declarations and predictions may be, they will certainly come to pass, unless the people are prepared for our new form of government by an education adapted to the new and peculiar situation of our country. To effect this great and necessary work let one of the first acts of the new Congress be to establish within the district to be allotted for them, a Federal university, into which the youth of the United States shall be received *after they have finished their studies and taken degrees in the colleges of their respective States.*

There, also, in the same year was the distinguished Samuel Blodget, author of the first American work on economic science, who, at the very beginning of a lifelong support of the proposition, briefly said :

> If a Federal university should be established . . . it must be simple, complete, and grand. . . . It must also be central, and under the patronage of the Federal power.

After these there followed a long line of advocates, beginning with the commissioners appointed under the " Act to establish the temporary and permanent seat of the Government of the United States," whose memorial to Congress on December 12, 1796, is especially worthy of attention, since, after referring to the setting apart of lands for a university site by Washington, and his having actually paid five thousand pounds sterling as a contribution toward the pecuniary foundation, the commissioners add the following :

> · They do not think it necessary to dilate on a subject in respect to which there seems to be but one voice. . . . We flatter ourselves it is only necessary to bring it within the view of the Federal legislature. We think you will eagerly seize the occasion to extend to it your patronage, to give birth to an institution which may perpetuate and endear your names to the latest posterity.

Then followed, in succeeding years : The friendly words of President John Adams in his inaugural address of March 4, 1797. The memorials of the resolute Samuel Blodget, especially the one of 1805, according to the Annals of Congress " representing that subscriptions toward a university at Washington have already been made to the number of eighteen thousand, and a sum received amounting to $30,000."

The efforts of Thomas Jefferson on many occasions, especially in his sixth annual message of December 2, 1806, in which, after offering abundant reasons in support of Washington's views, he added :

> The present consideration of a national establishment for education, particularly, is rendered proper by this circumstance also, that if Congress, approving the proposition, shall yet think it more eligible to found it on a donation of lands, they have it now in their power to endow it with those which will be among the earliest to

produce the necessary income. This foundation would have the advantage of being independent in war, which may suspend other improvements by requiring for its own purposes the resources destined for them.

The like earnest support of President James Madison in —
(1) His second message, of December 5, 1810, showing that "such an institution . . . would be universal in its beneficial effects;"
(2) His seventh annual message, of December 15, 1815, in which he said: "Such an institution deserves the patronage of Congress as a memorial of that solicitude for the advancement of knowledge without which the blessings of liberty cannot be fully enjoyed or long preserved;"
(3) His last annual message, of December 3, 1816, wherein again he forcibly urged "the establishment of a national university within the District on a scale and for objects worthy of the American nation."  •

The efforts of President James Monroe, in coöperation with others, for the development of the Columbian Institute, in the hope of its becoming eventually the desired national university.

The eloquent appeals in this behalf by President John Quincy Adams in both messages and speeches, especially in his first message (1825), so sound in its reasoning, so pathetic in its allusions to Washington, and so full of deserved reproach for his fellow-countrymen:

So convinced of this [the need of a national university] was the first of my predecessors in this office, now first in the memory, as he was first in the hearts of his countrymen, that once and again, in his addresses to the Congresses with whom he coöperated in the public service, he earnestly recommended the establishment of seminaries of learning, to prepare for all the emergencies of peace and war, a national university, and a military academy. With respect to the latter, had he lived to the present day, in turning his eyes to the institution at West Point he would have enjoyed the gratification of his most earnest wishes. But in surveying the city which has been honored with his name he would have seen the spot of earth which he had destined and bequeathed to the use and benefit of his country as the site for a university still bare and barren. '

The subsequent efforts of earnest men both in and out of Congress, among them such men as the eloquent President

Holley, of Kentucky, and the learned Judge William Cranch, until the coming of Andrew Jackson, who so gladly approved of further Congressional aid in the form of $25,000 cash to Columbian College, in 1832, on account of the acknowledged " utility of a central literary establishment," and of the failure thus far to make any more direct recognition of the repeated recommendations of his predecessors.

Thenceforward for a period of forty years there was silence on the part of the presidents and of Congress. The several executives had become disheartened by the inability of the national legislature to rise to a comprehension of the needs of American education. Not so its friends among the people, for these four decades of comparative darkness were studded with starry names, like those of —

President Thomas Hill, of Harvard,
Professor Benjamin Peirce, of Cambridge,
Professor Louis Agassiz, of Cambridge,
Dr. James Apthorp Gould, astronomer,
Professor John F. Norton, of Yale,
Professor James Hall, geologist, of New York,
Professor Amos Dean, of Albany,
Bishop Alonzo Potter, of New York,
President James McCosh, of Princeton,
Professor Arnold Guyot, of Princeton,
Professor Joseph Henry, of the Smithsonian Institution,
Professor O. M. Mitchell, Director of the Cincinnati Observatory,
Dr. Alexander Dallas Bache, Superintendent of the Coast Survey,
and so on.

But all these were the individual appeals of illustrious men. There was need of organization. And so in 1869, on motion of Dr. John W. Hoyt, of Wisconsin, the National Educational Association espoused the cause and formed a great committee for its furtherance. Three successive annual reports, in which were set forth the need of a central university of highest rank and the principles which should govern in its organization, were unanimously approved by the Association, and a bill was finally prepared in counsel with Senators Sumner, Patterson, Howe, and others, and introduced in both Houses of Congress, and by the House Committee on Education unanimously reported in 1873.

President Ulysses S. Grant, having meanwhile become

deeply interested in the cause, gave it his indorsement in characteristic manner, as follows:

I would suggest to Congress the propriety of promoting the establishment in this District of an institution of learning or university of the highest class, by donation of lands. There is no place better suited for such an institution than the national capital. There is no other place in which every citizen is so directly interested.

Unfortunately, for reasons known to those directly interested, the National Educational Association, having fulfilled the service of reënforcing the old demand, and of indicating the scope and outline of the proposed university, did not systematically persist in its efforts with Congress for a considerable time thereafter.

But the advocacy of the proposition went forward under the individual lead of strong men in all sections of the country — such men as —

Senator Charles Sumner, of Massachusetts,
Senator Timothy O. Howe, of Wisconsin,
Senator J. W. Patterson, of New Hampshire,
Senator Carl Schurz, of Wisconsin and New York,
General John Eaton, National Commissioner of Education,
Dr. William T. Harris, editor *Journal of Speculative Philosophy* and present National Commissioner of Education,
President Daniel Read, University of Missouri,
President James C. Welling, Columbian University,
Mr. E. L. Godkin, Editor of *The Nation*,
President D. F. Boyd, University of Louisiana,
President Andrew D. White, Cornell University,
President James B. Angell, University of Michigan, and many others.

Meanwhile, came the messages of Rutherford B. Hayes, in 1877 and 1878, arguing the case with a cogency and eloquence unsurpassed, and concluding thus:

The Government cannot now repudiate or reverse its beneficent educational policy. The logic of facts and of reason will not permit it to stop short of the most complete provision for every department of American education. The people are growing in their realization of the necessity there is for insuring the best possible education of the masses. The variety and vastness of the national resources, and the rapid progress of other nations, are making a strong and growing demand upon the industrial arts, which they are powerless to meet without the help of the best technical schools; while the conspicuous place we hold among the great nations of the earth, the nature of our Government, and the genius and aspirations of our people are reasons deep and urgent for a high and thorough culture that must early move the nation to adopt measures that will give to the United States a true university.

Also, in 1885, came the equivalent of a Presidential message in the annual report of Hon. L. Q. C. Lamar, Secretary of the Interior, eloquently insisting that President Jefferson was right when he "told Congress that to complete the circle of democratic policy a national university was a necessity and should at once be created;" that, while " the common-school system . . . constitutes the foundation of our democracy . . . this is not enough to satisfy its instincts; " and that the means of the highest possible culture " will alone realize and express the higher aspirations of American democracy."

Finally, in 1890, there was another beginning of work in Congress by Senator George F. Edmunds's offer of " A Bill to establish the University of the United States," and the creation of a select committee of nine senators to have charge of this interest during that Congress; which committee, having been twice continued, was at length made a standing committee, and has submitted three successive reports, two of them unanimous.

So likewise, in 1891, there was a resumption of organized effort outside of Congress, to-wit:

(1) By action of the Human Freedom League on the occasion of its organization in Independence Hall, Philadelphia, on October 11 of that year, under inspiration of an eloquent paper on " The Nation's Debt of Honor," by Dr. G. Brown Goode, of the Smithsonian Institution.

(2) By the General Committee of Three Hundred of the Pan-Republic Congress, in adopting a set of resolutions offered by John.W. Hoyt, on October 13, 1891, and by the appointment of a committee including one member from each of the States, to promote the enterprise.

(3) By the " Memorial in regard to a National University," by John W. Hoyt, printed in large edition by order of the United States Senate.

(4) By the introduction of National University bills of the aforesaid committee's preparation, in both houses of Con-

gress, and the securing of reports thereon by the Senate Select Committee.

(5) By the formation, in November, 1895, of a great and independent committee of citizens, to be known as "The National University Committee of One Hundred to promote the establishment of the University of the United States," a committe since grown to be one of over three hundred, including many of our most distinguished scholars, scientists, jurists, and statesmen, the presidents of some one hundred and fifty of our principal universities and colleges, and the State superintendents of public instruction in all the States but one. For greater efficiency, it has an Executive Council composed of the following members :

The Hon. Melville W. Fuller, LL.D., Chief Justice of the United States,

Ex-U. S. Senator George F. Edmunds, LL.D., of Vermont,

Ex-Provost William Pepper, M.D., LL.D., University of Pennsylvania,

Hon. Andrew D. White, LL.D., Ex-President of Cornell University, Ex-U. S. Minister to Russia, etc., New York,

Ex-Governor John Lee Carroll, LL.D., General President Society of Sons of the Revolution, Maryland,

General Horace Porter, LL.D., President-General Society of Sons of the American Revolution, New York,

Ex-U. S. Senator Eppa Hunton, LL.D., Virginia,

Ex-U. S. Senator A. H. Garland, late Attorney-General of the United States, Arkansas,

Ex-U. S. Senator J. B. Henderson, LL.D., Missouri and District of Columbia,

Colonel Wilbur R. Smith, Kentucky University,

General John Eaton, LL.D., Ex-U. S. Commissioner of Education, etc., New Hampshire and the District of Columbia,

Hon. Gardiner G. Hubbard, LL.D., President National Geographic Society, Regent of Smithsonian Institution, etc., District of Columbia,

Dr. Simon Newcomb, LL.D., etc., Director of the Nautical Almanac, District of Columbia,

Hon. John A. Kasson, Ex-U. S. Minister to Austria and Ambassador to Germany, Iowa and the District of Columbia,

Hon. Oscar S. Strauss, Ex-U. S. Minister to Turkey, New York,

Ex-Governor John W. Hoyt, M.D., LL.D., Chairman of National University Committees.

(6) By the introduction, in both Houses of Congress, of a new bill prepared by the Executive Council in November, 1895 (all members being present but one).

(7) By the arguments of nearly all members of the Council in support of the bill, before the Senate and House Committees, during the month of January, 1896; which bill has since been favorably reported.

The Senate has not yet taken up and passed any bill, for in each case the reports thereon have been submitted too late to admit of action; but that body has ever shown a friendly and liberal spirit, printing the following documents upon request, some of them in editions of several thousands, copies of which may be obtained on application to John W. Hoyt, Chairman, etc., 4 Iowa Circle, Washington, D. C.

The Bill submitted by Senator Edmunds, in 1890.

The Bill submitted by Senator Proctor, in 1891.

The "Memorial in regard to a National University," by John W. Hoyt, in 1892, containing both a full discussion of the National University proposition, and an exhaustive summary of the notable efforts made in this behalf from before the foundation of the Government.

The Report of the Senate Committee, submitted by Chairman Proctor, in 1893.

The Report of the Senate Committee, submitted by Chairman Hunton, in 1894.

The Speeches in support of the measure, delivered by Senators Hunton of Virginia, Vilas of Wisconsin, and Kyle of South Dakota.

The Bill prepared by the National University Committee of One Hundred.

The Report of the Senate Committee, on the said Bill, submitted by Senator Kyle, in 1896, including the arguments before the Committee by nearly all members of the Executive Council, as well as letters in support of the measure from over three hundred distinguished men in all sections of the country.

"Views of the Minority," submitted by Senator Walthall of Mississippi, in 1896.

"Reply to Views of the Minority," by John W. Hoyt.

The Argument in behalf of the National University proposition, by Professor William H. H. Phillips, of South Dakota, in December, 1896.

The Argument in support of the measure by President David Starr Jordan, of Leland Stanford University, in December, 1896.

The present movement, both in and out of Congress, is based upon the principles laid down and the reasons urged in the reports of the National Educational Association, and in the Senate Memorial of 1892.

In order that the purpose cherished, the principles agreed upon, the considerations which have led to a renewal of effort, and the conditions of success may clearly appear, extracts from an Outline of the Memorial will next be presented.

From the Outline, these passages, to-wit:

I. A great and true University the leading want of American education.

II. The offices of a National University are these :

    1. To supplement existing institutions by supplying full courses of post-graduate instruction, and it only, in every department of learning.

    2. By its central faculties and cluster of professional schools of highest grade, to represent at all times the sum of human knowledge.

    3. To lead in the upbuilding of new professions by its applications of science.

    4. To lead the world in the work of research and investigation.

III. Reasons why the Government should establish such a University :

    1. Neither existing institutions nor the great denominational universities in prospect can meet the demand. The nation only is equal to the founding of such a university as the nation needs.

    2. The Government needs the influence of a National University.

    3. The American system of education can only be made complete by the crowning university it lacks, as a source of coördinating influence, inspiration, and elevating power.

    4. A National University would powerfully strengthen the patriotic sentiment of the country.

    5. A National University would more strongly than any other attract men of genius from every quarter of the world to its professorships and fellowships, thus increasing the cultured intellectual forces of both institution and country.

    6. A National University would especially attract students of high character from many lands, whose return after

years of contact with free institutions would promote the cause of liberal government everywhere.

7. The founding of a National University would be, therefore, a most fitting thing for a great nation ambitious to lead the world in civilization.

IV. Reasons for founding such University at Washington :

1. Washington was designated by the Father of his Country in his bequest of property in aid of its endowment and by his selection of land for a site.

2. Washington is the only sufficient and convenient spot where the Government has both exclusive and perpetual jurisdiction.

3. There are in the Government departments, and connected therewith, vast amounts of material which could be made auxiliary, and which, being now but partially utilized, are in some part a capital of thirty millions of dollars running to waste.

4. There are hundreds of experts in the departments whose services could be more or less utilized with mutual advantage.

5. Such a university in Washington would exert a great influence upon the National Government itself, in every branch and department.

VI. Reasons for a renewal of the effort for a National University at this time :

1. The need not only remains, but increases with the years, as shown by the fact that some three thousand American graduates are now seeking opportunities abroad.

2. Since this need can only be met by the nation, why not *begin now ?*

3. No other important educational measure is now likely to interfere.

4. A beginning now on the part of the National Government would be certain to attract large donations from private sources for the endowment of fellowships, professorships, faculties, and departments.

5. The growing power of the United States among the nations suggests the corresponding present need of such forces and influences at the seat of Government as shall be worthy to impress and lead the world.

VII. The proposition of to-day is this :

To urge upon Congress the early establishment of a National University of the highest type, and to be known as the University of the United States,

Whose form of constitution shall secure it against partisan control, a thing not difficult, as shown by the success of leading State universities and of scientific institutions controlled by the General Government.

Whose internal management shall be with its educational members.

Whose conditions of admission shall be character and competency.

Whose applicants for degrees already have the bachelor's degree.

Whose fellowships shall be duly endowed and open to the best qualified.

Whose professoriate shall be so constituted as to secure to it the highest possible character and efficiency.

Whose departments of letters, science, and philosophy shall be centres for the grouping of post-graduate professional schools of every class.

Whose beginnings shall be with such means as befit the great undertaking, and shall encourage liberal endowments from other than governmental sources; thus early making it the leading university of the world.

As in part said before, the conditions of success in this movement are these:

First, they who are in power must give the matter its full measure of consideration. Absorbed in other matters, pressed by measures of finance, commerce, lands, industrial development, and much else, even the most intelligent and large-minded of men are in danger of overlooking a measure, however important, comprehensive, and far-reaching, that is neither vital to party success nor boldly insists on being heard.

Secondly, while it may be assumed that such of our statesmen as already appreciate the importance of the enterprise, seeing clearly how it would promote the national welfare and advance the cause of learning in the world, are equal to the responsibility of taking it up, it is but right as well as desirable that they be duly reënforced by the enlightened sentiment of the country. And they certainly will be.

Educators at the head of our schools, academies, colleges, and universities, with the multitude of their friends, none of whom can fail to see the incalculable value of a crowning institution like the one proposed, will in yet greater numbers join hands for its early realization when they discover an earnest purpose in Congress.

The press of the United States, so liberal and ever on the alert for new measures of progress, has already done much, and can safely be counted on to more fully interest the general public in a proposition so often urged by the Father of his Country, so repeatedly indorsed by other statesmen in all periods of the national history, and so clearly a condition of the highest dignity and welfare of the Republic. Aye, patriotic Americans in general must reënforce the great army already enlisted, unfurling banners not to be furled until the victory is fully won.

Objections have been raised by the heads of a half-dozen ambitious institutions, old, new, and on paper; but they have been answered, and need not be again discussed, unless they should reappear. Such opposition as may manifest itself in any form will disappear on a nearer, more scrutinizing, and broader view.

There has not been named in all the past, nor can there be named in any future, one argument against the National University proposition of George Washington that will bear the scrutiny of philosophy or the test of history.

Let the purpose be unalterably fixed that ere the centennial of his last effort and bequest, the ninth day of July, 1899, the Government of the United States shall have taken the long anticipated decisive step in this great behalf. Let the watch-word of Americans everywhere be, The crowning university proposed by George Washington, recommended by the most illustrious of his successors, as well as urged by a long line of other distinguished citizens, and still the crying need of American education — the University of the United States — must be established without further delay. Joining with the distinguished and lamented Gould, of Cambridge and Córdoba, astronomer of two hemispheres, let us say, as with one voice: Found the University. It shall be, first of all, for Americans and the honor of America, but also for the advancement of knowledge and freedom everywhere. " Found it, and throngs of European youth will also crowd its halls, carrying back with them American ideas to ennoble their own lands, bringing hither with them counterpoises of transatlantic thought that shall ennoble ours, and both by their coming and their going cementing the family of nations in bonds of mutual sympathy and attachment. Found it, though it cost the whole revenues of a capital. Let earth, air, and sea bring their tribute; let California and India pour in their gold, and the busy marts of men their gains, till this great work is done. Thus shall we achieve the glory of a nation, the welfare of a continent, the advancement of the race, and crown the clustering hopes of humanity with more than full fruition."

IN THE SENATE OF THE UNITED STATES.

MARCH 3, 1893.—Ordered to be printed.

Mr. PROCTOR, from the Select Committee to Establish the University of the United States, submitted the following

# REPORT:

[To accompany S. 3824.]

The Select Committee to Establish the University of the United States, to whom was referred the bill (S. 3824) to establish a national university, having considered the same, report:

The value of knowledge is recognized in all civilized countries, but in no country does it deserve higher recognition than in our own, for our Government is founded upon it, and we need it everywhere and all forms of it for our highest development. Hitherto there has been practical recognition of this in the United States in providing for State universities, for schools of agriculture and the mechanic arts, for military and naval schools, for the Department of Agriculture and the different surveys, and for great libraries. It is the purpose of this bill to make such organization more complete and more worthy of a great and progressive people by creating at the capital of the nation one supreme-institution that (1) shall complete the system of American education by supplying the crowning and true university it lacks, both as a means of furnishing upon American soil every possible facility for the highest available culture, and of exciting a stimulating and elevating influence upon all classes of schools of lower rank; (2) that shall bring together in friendly as well as high intellectual intercourse a large number of the most gifted and aspiring representatives of all the States for the pursuit of the highest knowledge in all departments of learning; thus supplying in endless succession the best trained thinkers and workers for every field of intellectual activity, with broader views of men and things, as well as increased love of country and a juster regard for the citizens thereof, irrespective of locality, and more certainly assuring to the United States their proper place in the forefront of advancing nations.

That there has ever been in the past a deep realization of our deficiencies in this field is manifest:

First. From the great number of the ambitious young men of the country who, from the beginning, have been accustomed to go abroad for opportunities they could not find at home.

Second. From the zealous and repeated efforts of many of the foremost scholars, scientists, and statesmen to have in this country at least one post-graduate university of the highest possible grade.

Third. From the many honorable, but still inadequate, efforts of existing institutions, and of large-minded, philanthropic men to meet this demand by increase of endowments devoted to proper university work.

Fourth. From the strong declarations repeatedly made by individual citizens and organized bodies of men most competent to judge, that when all shall have been done that can be through individual and denominational agencies, it will still be the high duty and interest of the nation itself to establish and liberally endow an institution of such rank as is proposed by this bill.

Such an institution only could in any proper sense complete the now incomplete system of American education and most wisely direct all worthy efforts in the field of original research and utilize the facilities for it so rapidly accumulating at Washington.

Such an institution only could possibly become the long-deferred realization of the aspirations and official appeals of those profoundly wise founders of the Republic, some of whom not only outlined the principles upon which it should be established, and the relations it should sustain to the Government and people, but, also, devised for it sources of revenue, and set apart lands of the District of Columbia deemed suitable for the location of its buildings.

The proposed bill is intended to represent and give fruition to the plans and desires of Washington, Jefferson, Madison, and other Presidents, together with a multitude of citizens in other high stations. It was prepared with the concurrence of citizens most competent to advise in such matters; and not only the ends sought to be attained, but also the means and agencies to be employed have received the sanction of many of the foremost scholars and statesmen of all portions of the country.

It provides for the establishment of a university of the highest type, resting upon the State universities and other institutions of collegiate rank as they rest upon the high schools and academies—a university whose facilities shall be open to all who are competent to use them, but whose degrees shall be conferred upon such only as have already received a degree from some institution recognized by the university authorities; whose opportunities are to be open without price to qualified representatives from every State and Congressional district of the United States; whose several departments shall have endowed fellowships, open to persons of genius from whatever quarter of the world, for the advancement of knowledge by means of original researches; to whose professors, fellows, and students, all government collections, literary, scientific, and practical, are to be freely open without detriment to the public service; and whose several heads of departments are to have advisory and coöperative relations with the heads of Government bureaus for the mutual advantage of the Government itself and the cause of universal science.

The plan of government for the university seems well calculated to keep the institution in close relation with the people of all sections and yet safe from the dangers of political interference, while at the same time leaving the internal affairs and whatever is most vital to its welfare in the hands of those who are at once most competent to manage them and have the largest stake in its prosperity.

As a partial provision for the location of the necessary buildings the bill grants the site selected for this purpose by President Washington in 1796, and now, since the removal of the Naval Observatory, without important use; and for the support of the institution sets apart one-half the net proceeds of the public lands, one-half of such half to be used currently in providing for the opening of the institution and for carrying it on, the remainder to accumulate in the Treasury of the United States as an endowment until competent to yield a sufficient revenue, together with the gifts and bequests that may be attracted to it, for the permanent support of the institution.

Your committee are of the opinion that the cause of American learning demands such an institution as this bill provides for; that the highest dignity and welfare of the nation demand it; that it should be established at the capital of the country; and that after a delay of one hundred years since it was first proposed and sought to be established by the founders of the Government it would be unworthy of so great a people to wait longer for a more favorable time in which to meet all these high demands.

The committee, therefore, unanimously approve the bill and recommend its passage.

A BILL to establish a national university.

*Be it enacted by the Senate and House of Representatives of the United States of America in Congress assembled,* That an institution shall be, and is hereby, established in the District of Columbia, to be called "The University of the United States," where instruction shall be given in the higher branches of all departments of knowledge, practical as well as literary and scientific, and where facilities shall be furnished for research and investigation.

SEC. 2. That the government of the university shall be vested in a board of regents and a council of faculties.

SEC. 3. That the board of regents shall consist of one member from each State of the United States, to be appointed by the governor thereof, with the concurrence of the chief justice and the chief educational officer of his State; six members to be appointed by the President of the United States, with the advice and consent of the Senate; the following members ex officio, to wit, the President of the United States, who shall be honorary president of the board, the Vice-President of the United States, the Chief Justice of the United States, the Speaker of the House of Representatives, the Commissioner of Education, the Secretary of the Smithsonian Institution, and the president of the university; fifteen to be a quorum. The regents and their successors are hereby created a body politic and corporate, with the name of "The Regents of the University of the United States," and with power, subject to limitations herein prescribed, to adopt statutes for the government of the university, to elect the officers thereof, to determine the conditions of admission to the university, to confer such degrees, and such only, as are recommended by the council of faculties, and in general to perform any and all acts not inconsistent herewith or with the Constitution and laws of the United States which may be necessary to the ends herein proposed.

SEC. 4. That the first meeting of the board of regents shall be called by the President of the United States, and shall be held in the city of Washington within three months after the passage of this act. At such meeting all members representing the several States shall be divided, as nearly as possible, into six equal classes, such division being according to an alphabetical arrangement of the States by them represented. The classes thus formed shall be numbered in the order of such arrangement, and shall retire in such order at the end of one, two, three, four, five, and six years, respectively, and their successors shall be appointed thereafter for the term of six years. If the governor of any State shall neglect to make such appointment within three months after the notice of a vacancy for such State the board may fill the same by the election of some suitable citizen thereof. The regents first appointed by the President shall retire in the order of their names on the list of appointments at the end of one, two, three, four, five, and six years, and their successors thereafter shall be appointed for the term of six years. In order to the fullest efficiency the board of regents shall designate seven of its members, including the president of the university as chairman ex officio, to act as an executive committee, with authority to choose the members of faculties and all employees of the university and fix their compensation, as well as to transact ordinary current business, and to perform such other duties as are imposed. The six members appointed shall be chosen for one, two, three, four, five, and six years, respectively, and their successors shall be appointed for the term of six years.

Meetings of the board shall be held annually for the transaction of general business and the conferring of degrees. Special meetings may also be held upon call of the executive committee as the exigencies of the university shall require.

SEC. 5. That the chief officer of the university shall be a president chosen by the board of regents and hold office during their pleasure. He shall be president of the board of regents and of the council of faculties, shall have general supervision of the university, and discharge such other duties as are prescribed by the board or by the council of faculties. The treasurer of the university shall also be appointed by the regents, and give bonds approved by them. He shall perform the duties usually required of such officers and such other duties as are imposed by the board of regents.

SEC. 6. That the council of faculties, embracing the president of the university and all heads of faculties, shall be charged with the planning and direction of instruction and discipline in the several departments, and with the other duties prescribed in the statutes or designated by the regents.

SEC. 7. That the immediate government of each faculty shall be intrusted to its own members. Its chairman, to be known as dean of the faculty, shall be chosen by the executive committee on the recommendation of the president of the university, and shall be responsible for the supervision of its internal affairs.

SEC. 8. That no chair for instruction sectarian in religion or partisan in politics shall be maintained upon funds derived from the general university endowment, or permitted in any form, and no sectarian or partisan test shall be allowed in the appointment of professors to the chairs so endowed and maintained, or in the selection of any officer of the university; but chairs of faculties for instruction in any department of learning may be endowed by gift, devise, or bequest, and the parties endowing the same, or their legally authorized trustees, shall have the privilege, subject to the approval of the board of regents, of designating the titles thereof and the instruction to which such endowments shall be devoted. No amount less than one hundred thousand dollars, however, shall be considered a full endowment for any chair in the university. Existing institutions, which are free from controlling obligations of a sectarian or partisan nature, and have endowments sufficient to support a faculty, may, with the approval of the regents, and on terms prescribed by them, become faculties or departments of the university, still retaining or adopting such titles as they may prefer.

Sec. 9. That the facilities afforded by the university shall be open to all who are competent to use them, on conditions prescribed by the executive committee, with the advice of the faculties and officers directly concerned; but degrees shall be conferred upon such persons only as shall have previously received the degree of bachelor of arts, or an equivalent degree, from some institution recognized for this purpose by the university authorities.

Sec. 10. That in order to extend the privileges of the university and to improve the collegiate and other grades of public instruction in the country, it is provided that each State and Territory of the United States, in the ratio of population, shall be entitled to free scholarships of such number, not less than one for each Representative and Delegate in Congress and two for each Senator, as the board of regents shall determine. The executive committee of the board of regents may, for sufficient reasons, withhold the award of any scholarship, or cancel its privileges or those of any student in the university.

Sec. 11. That for the advancement of science and learning by means of researches and investigations, there shall be established fellowships in the university of such character and number as the interests to be represented and the resources at command shall warrant; which fellowships shall yield a partial or a full support, as the regents shall determine. They may be provided for out of the university income, or may be endowed by gift or otherwise, and the persons, organizations, corporate bodies, or States endowing them may, subject to the approval of the board of regents. designate their titles and the researches or investigations they shall be used to encourage.

Sec. 12. That in the admission and appointment of persons to places in the university, character and competency shall be the sole test of qualifications.

Sec. 13. That as a means of partially providing building sites for the several departments of the university, the following tract of land, selected and appropriated by President Washington for the site of the national university proposed by him, and in part actually endowed by provisions of his last will and testament, to wit, that tract in the city of Washington long known as "University Square," and now occupied by the National Observatory, is hereby granted and set apart for the use and benefit of the university of the United States when no longer required for observatory purposes.

Sec. 14. That for the practical establishment, support, and maintenance of the university, there is hereby appropriated and set apart one-half the net proceeds of the sales of the public lands, as the same shall accrue from year to year. Of this amount, one-half shall be held by the Treasurer of the United States for use in securing and improving grounds for the seat of the university, for providing the necessary buildings and equipments, and for conducting the institution after its opening; but the remaining one-half shall be allowed to accumulate in the Treasury as a permanent fund, yielding interest at the rate of five per centum per annum as a further revenue, until such fund, together with the endowments from other sources, shall be sufficient for the support of the university, after which all the net proceeds of the sales of public lands so used for university purposes shall be passed to the general fund or otherwise used, as Congress shall determine. All moneys held by the Treasurer of the United States under the provisions of this act shall be subject to requisitions drawn, as may be necessary, by the president and secretary of the board of regents under its order, but with this limitation, namely, that after the first five years subsequent to the organization of the board, not more than ten per centum of the aforementioned proceeds available for the erection of buildings and providing equipments shall be so used in any one year.

SEC. 15. That the board of regents shall have power to receive and administer all such gifts, devises, and bequests as are made for the benefit of the university; which gifts, devises, and bequests, if in money, shall be deposited with the Treasurer of the United States, who shall pay interest thereon quarterly at the rate of 5 per centum per annum.

SEC. 16. That after the formal opening of the university for instruction the members thereof, under rules approved by the officers, subject to any regulations prescribed by Congress, shall have access to all institutions, collections, and opportunities for study and research under control of the Government, so far as the same can be accorded without detriment to the public service; and to the end that all such facilities may be utilized to the fullest extent and that the Government service may in turn derive the largest benefit from the work done in the university, the heads of all bureaus, institutions, and other organizations of the Government, whose work is of a sort to justify it, shall be by the executive committee of the board brought into such advisory and co-operative relations with the heads of corresponding departments of the university as such committee, with the advice of the heads of faculties and the aforesaid officers of the Government, shall agree upon as being advantageous.

SEC. 17. That at the close of the fiscal year the board of regents shall make a report to Congress, showing the operations, condition, and wants of the university; one copy of which shall be transmitted free to all institutions of learning endowed by the Government under any act of Congress, and to all other institutions of learning in the United States whose degrees are recognized by this university.

www.ingramcontent.com/pod-product-compliance
Lightning Source LLC
Chambersburg PA
CBHW031439280326
41927CB00038B/985